Lucky
Enough

To David

Semper Fi

Edith Basler

"Since recording *Tie a Yellow Ribbon* in 1973 and singing it live to the POWs from Vietnam, Cambodia and Laos at the Cotton Bowl in Dallas and to this day entertaining the troops in Afghanistan and Iraq, I have read many books on veterans and the military. **Lucky Enough** is a must read. Eddie Beesley makes you feel proud to be an American." ~ *Tony Orlando*

"Lucky Enough is a concise, personal description of the courage, initiative and mental stamina which enables an individual to overcome the most serious of adversities. **Lucky Enough** should be read by every American and become an important part of the mosaic which makes our country great." ~ *Henry Bellmon, Former Governor and US Senator and World War II Marine*

"**Lucky Enough** is the compelling story of a seventeen year old boy whose life is forever sculpted by the Vietnam War. But more than that, it is a story of courage, perseverance and hope. Spellbinding." ~ *Linda Cavanaugh, Anchor/Reporter, KFOR-TV*

"**Lucky Enough** is not a war story, but a LIFE story that is still on-going. It's a story filled with love, commitment, dedication and patriotism. Eddie Beesley certainly did not choose the hand that was dealt him, but he is playing it to the best of his ability, and it looks like he is winning." ~ *Len Zaborowski, Army Security Agency, Korea, 1955-1956*

Lucky Enough

by
Eddie R. Beesley

River Road Press
Laguna Vista, TX

Published by River Road Press,
an imprint of Red Engine Press

Library of Congress Control Number: 2005934990

ISBN – 10: 0-9663276-7-5
ISBN – 13: 978-0-9663276-7-0

Cover illustration by Brandi Alltizer
Edited by Personalized Literary Services

Printed in the United States of America

Third Printing - 2014

Quantity discounts are available on bulk purchases of this book for
educational institutions or social organizations, For information,
please contact the publisher:
River Road Press
13 Torrey Pines Drive
Laguna Vista, TX 78578

Acknowledgments

To the Beesley family, I am blessed and highly favored to be one of you.

To the Gaudette family, you have received me with great love and respect.

To Teresa, Eddie, James, Lila and grandchildren, there are no words to express the great joy you bring to my life.

To Jan, Erin and family, you have a place in my life no one else can fill.

But most of all Connie, you have stood by my side through the heartbreak of shattered dreams and have been there to share the joys of dreams fulfilled. Since that day we first met, you have been, and still are, the center of my universe. Thank you for being my wife, lover and friend.

Lucky Enough

Foreword

At last! Ed started this book as we drove toward the Wall[1] in August of 1995. I had asked him to record some of what he was feeling to help our children and grandchildren know and better understand the Marine in him. Although I grew up knowing what our servicemen go through, our children have had different life experiences. I wanted them to know the price of freedom.

When I met Ed, I was working as a USO[2] hostess. As it got harder for me to meet the guys being shipped out, I decided to visit the men who were in the hospital. I was homesick for my parents and being around military personnel at the hospital felt good to me. I took cookies and magazines to the patients, sat with them – talked to them.

It wasn't easy to see all the injuries, but I don't remember crying or feeling pity for any of them. I did feel a great sense of loss – especially with the amputees like Ed. Most of them were in good to fair moods – not bitter. I wanted to help, to be there for them – to let them know how much I cared about them and their service to our country. I still feel that way. That is why I write so many letters to our servicemen and women whenever there is any conflict going on, and when I can get addresses.

When Ed and I made that first trip to Washington to visit the Wall, I was emotional too. My father was a Navy Corpsman. He died from a heart attack brought

---

1   The Vietnam War Memorial in Washington D. C.
2   USO – United Service Organization

on by the stress of caring for the young men coming back from the Vietnam War. He was dedicated to serving his country and those in the military. As Ed approached the Wall, I thought about my dad and all those lost in this and other wars. I thought about their families and the sorrow that never ends. You see that infinite grief in the pictures and notes left behind for those whose names are on the Wall. I once saw a sonogram with a note, "This is your grandchild."

I knew this would be hard for Ed. I also knew that he had to do a part of it on his own. He knew he could talk to me and that I would have some understanding, but he also knew that I would respect his privacy and give him space at the Wall. He needed to do this. I was glad to be there with him – to be a part of it. I was also glad that our grandson Dillon was there to share it with him.

Back when I accepted Ed's marriage proposal there were those who were concerned that it was because I felt sorry for him. How could that be? This handsome young man had a zest for life and it was obvious to me that he was someone very special. I was right. He has been my strength, my rock, my hero, my knight in shining armor. I have lived much of this story with him and even I am awed with his courage. He has been an inspiration to me and many others and I believe his story will continue to inspire.

Connie Beesley, August 2005

THE CALL OF THE WALL -- August 29, 1995

Marines don't cry, but sometimes their eyes sweat.

The alarm sounds at 6:30 A.M. I open my eyes and see a photograph of a handsome young Marine Lance Corporal on the wall near my bed. A set of U.S. and Marine Corps flags, a stuffed Marine bulldog, special edition Marine Corps Coca-Cola cans and a statue of an American Bald Eagle sit on the shelf below the picture. A certificate of retirement from the U.S. Marine Corps and a certificate of promotion from Lance Corporal to Corporal hang nearby.

My wife springs out of bed to put on the coffee. I pull myself into a wheelchair and make my way to the bathroom. Tears fill my eyes as I see the reflection in the mirror. These are not tears of sorrow or even self-pity. They come from a mystical, almost spiritual connection between the image in the mirror and the proud young Marine in the photograph. I begin my morning routine the same as usual - but today is different. Today I will pay tribute to that nineteen-year-old boy who went off to war so long ago. Today I will remember Vietnam, where he put his life on the line. Today I will ponder the event that took both his legs and began an internal conflict that will continue for the rest of his life.

As I load the car and get ready for a trip to Washington D. C., a million thoughts race through my mind. I can't find words to express my feelings about visiting the Vietnam War Memorial, so I say little to my wife and family. On August 31, the thirtieth anniversary of the event that changed that young Marine forever, I want to be at the Wall. I close my eyes and imagine the long expanse of shiny black marble bearing the names of the fifty-eight thousand men and women who died (among them a nephew and many friends) in what some call a senseless war. There are others living in the shadow of Vietnam. I want to remember them too.

Most of all I want to say thank you to that young Marine for making me the son, the brother, the husband, the father and the grandfather that I have become. I am sure by now you have guessed that the young Marine in the picture, the image in the mirror and I, are one.

The car is loaded. Children ride past on their bicycles on the way to school. I raise my eyes to the sky and see Old Glory flying unfurled on the fla[...] front yard. Two of my grandchildren come o[...] them up and put them in the swing attached to th[...] of the walkway.

With Dillon and Ariel in the swing and Old Glory flying in the background, I have to stop and take a picture. I lift my eyes to heaven and whisper, "**Thank you God, that I am an American and please continue to bless America**." I wipe the tears from my eyes as we get in the car. We are on our way to Washington D. C.

Today it seems that I am less patient than usual. My thoughts and concerns turn inward. God gave me a wonderful wife who is very understanding. Connie is the daughter of a Navy Master Chief who served as a

ıg the Vietnam War. He was with
wa helping evacuate the wounded
he died of a massive heart attack.
he wall but he gave his life for his
w servicemen and women. Connie
t of freedom and its effect on not
ght for it but also their families,
ıes. Thank you God, and thank you,
Connie.

On the road with Connie driving, my grandson, Dillon, sleeps in the back seat. I so much appreciate our daughter, Teresa, for allowing Dillon to come with us. I would have liked to have all my children and grandchildren with me to share this very emotional time, but it could not be.

It seems as though the Monte Carlo knows where she is taking me. I don't understand it but some strange force is pulling me onward. I will not be satisfied until I reach my destination. I would drive through the night but Connie and Dillon are getting tired so we stop at a motel, eat dinner, go swimming and to the grocery store. We let Dillon ride the motorcycle outside the store, before going back to the room to eat grapes and watch Star Trek.

Childhood

I was the eighteenth of twenty-one children living on a farm in the small Oklahoma community of Nuyaka. Local legends say that a Creek Indian chief who visited the Big Apple named the town. Nuyaka was his pronunciation of New York. By today's standards, my family was very poor. Our house had no window panes and there were wide spaces between the boards of the outside walls. In the winter, we nailed sheet metal over the window openings and glued old papers inside the walls with flour and water paste. In warm weather, we children went barefoot. When it got cold, we wore second hand shoes. Our clothes were hand-me-downs sewn from flour sacks.

My parents were technically not sharecroppers, but many years a portion of the crops went to the landlord to pay the rent. My father worked the farm, rough necked in the oil fields and hired out to bale hay just to pay the grocery bill at the store and buy seed for the next year. My mother got up at 4:00 A.M., washed school clothes by hand and dried them on the wood stove, helped with the milking, fed the pigs and chickens and got the children off to school before my father got out of bed. She worked the fields, planted and tended a garden to feed the family, and cooked all the meals. Most of all, she was a close personal friend to Jesus and somehow none of her children ever remember going hungry. She always had a song, a poem or a comforting word. Long after everyone was in bed, she took time to talk to Jesus. Her prayers were the last thing we heard before we went to sleep. The sound of an old gospel hymn flowing from her lips was the first sound we heard in the morning - never a gripe or complaint. When she was ninety years old, I talked with her about the rough life she had lived. Her reply was, "Oh son, I have had a good life". I asked her where was I while you were having that *good life*?

I was always ready for adventure. When I was four or five, a group of Tulsa oilmen asked me to lead them to a lake deep in the woods to check out a drilling site. I'd only been there a couple of times with my family, but I was up to the challenge. When my older brothers were teaching me to swim in the Deep Fork River, I would beg "throw me in." When they tried to get my brother, Bill, to ride a wild young bull, I'd say, "Let me, let me. I can ride him." I did too - for a little while. I was the kid who would test a parachute his older brother built from a torn bed sheet and a five-gallon bucket by jumping off the barn. I guess it worked. I made it all the way to the ground, and boy, did I see stars.

My family spent a couple of years as migrant farm workers in Arizona and California, before returning to

Oklahoma and settling on a farm just outside Beggs, a small town about twenty-five miles south of Tulsa.

My childhood heroes were men like Davy Crockett and Daniel Boone. I fantasized about being an Indian scout. Forty-five years later, I learned that we are descended from Cherokee Indians. Some of our people were among the group of Cherokees driven to Oklahoma on the infamous "Trail Of Tears". Refusing imprisonment on a reservation, they escaped to hide out in the mountains of Arkansas and Missouri - passing themselves off as Black Dutch. I also found out that my mother's fifth cousin was General Stonewall Jackson.

As a young teen, my friend, Bobby, and I hung out on a river or stream with nothing but the clothes on our backs and our fishing poles. We spent days at a time living off what the earth provided. In junior high school, I participated in basketball and track. Of course, basketball was my first love. I was taller than the other boys in my class. I could jump higher, play harder and with more intensity than any one else. From the very first, I was a starter in every game.

From an early age I liked girls and they liked me. I loved flirting and showing off for them. I was good-looking and I knew it. Working on the farm and participating in sports had made my muscles sleek and well toned. I was especially proud of my thick shock of dark curly hair. Life was good.

As the high school years approached, things began to change. I became painfully aware of some of life's inequities. My sophomore year got off to a good start. Classes were good. My grades were good. Then came basketball season! I saw basketball as my ticket to a better education. I hoped to be the first in my family to graduate from college. As the season progressed, it became apparent that the coach was prepping two of his players for the college scouts, but I would not be one of them. I was bitterly disappointed.

My junior year was even more frustrating. The coach spent the majority of practice with his two golden boys and orchestrated our games to make them look good. Ironically, neither one of them attended college. I lost all interest in school when I realized there was no basketball scholarship in my future. There was no possible way my parents could pay for college.

It was tough giving up my dreams. Not having a goal left me feeling restless and unhappy. I knew that I had potential to be more than I was, but I couldn't find anyone to give me a chance. I needed a challenge. Something to bring out the inner person I knew I could be.

About two weeks before school was out for the year, my friend, Gary, and I skipped class and hitchhiked to Tulsa. As we walked down the street, we came to the Marine recruiting office. There in the window were pictures of young Marines in their dress blues that caught my eye. The uniform was the most beautiful in the world. The Marines were the toughest of the tough. Everything about the organization was top-notch as far as I could see. They offered the very thing I was seeking - adventure, a chance to compete, a future that was brighter than the one I faced if I stayed on the farm. I imagined myself as one of them - the few, the proud.

Thinking about how good I'd look in that uniform and how impressed the girls would be, I turned to Gary and said, "Let's join the Marines." We entered the office, talked to the recruiter and took the preliminary test. It turned out that Gary would have to wait three more months before he could join, and he ended up in the Army. However, that day my life changed forever.

Two weeks later, I was sworn in as a United States Marine in Oklahoma City. My mother wasn't enthusiastic about the idea, but my father signed for me. I was ecstatic. I was seventeen and I'd made my first adult decision. I was eager to begin the biggest adventure of my young life.

Of the two hundred men and women at the induction center in Oklahoma City that day, four joined the Marines. Two of them went home the first week of recruit training because of health problems. The other was a kid by the name of Charles Sides. He and I stuck it out and reached the pinnacle of achievement - we became United States Marines.

THE CALL OF THE WALL -- August 30, 1995

Pain Is Only Temporary, Pride Is Forever

Connie is driving now. We are somewhere east of Indianapolis. I have always pretty much kept it all together but if Connie could read my thoughts at this moment, she would think I've lost my mind.

I see myself as a Marine corporal - the one beside the picture in the dictionary when you look up Combat Marine. He is tan from the scorching Vietnamese summer sun and hard as a rock from extensive survival and Marine Raider training. He is a Marine's Marine, his shirt tucked neatly into his bloused trousers and his campaign cover[4] turned up on the left side to display the word Vietnam. A thin mustache streaks across his upper lip.

I see a boot lieutenant shouting orders to a group of tired young men. The corporal grabs him with both hands by the shirt collar as the lieutenant yells, "I'll have your stripes for this. I am Lieutenant Somebody". Getting in the man's face, the corporal replies, "I don't care who you are. These are MY men. If you want them to do something, you go through me."

This vision brings back memories of this same young corporal on patrol with his men. They begin to fall out from the heat and exhaustion. I see the corporal giving his men water from his canteen. Grabbing the

---

4 Cloth hat.

10

boys with his free hand, he slings their packs and weapons over one shoulder and they continue with their mission. His close friends call him "Guts and Hack It".

I think about Lieutenant Mitchell. Right from the beginning, there was something special about him. He reminded me of my brother, Gene, who was killed when I was sixteen - right before I went into the Marines.

In the military, enlisted personnel and officers don't fraternize. Lieutenant Mitchell and I could never have been buddies because of that - but we shared the same attitude toward the Corps. We wanted to look good - to be the best at what we did. I felt like he trusted me and I wanted to live up to that trust.

I remember the nights in Vietnam – guarding our perimeter when the Lieutenant came around to talk with my friend, Norm Kegerreis, and me. I remember him talking about his new baby. I remember – showers to remove the grunge accumulated from weeks of hard, hot, sweating details.

They told us that when we landed at Chu Lai, it would be the first beach landing since Korea. Prepared for significant opposition from the North Vietnamese Regular Army, we went in on Amtracks[5]. The trax stopped and let down the ramps in waist deep water.

_____
5   Amphibious Tractors, also called trax.

We were already soaked with seawater that flooded the trax when they went off the LSD[6]. We waded ashore and hit the sand. The combination of seawater, salt and sand was miserable.

We had to wear it for about a week and a half until one of our patrols took us across a river. The water was so inviting. We stripped to our skivvies and jumped in. Within minutes, one of the guys began screaming as if he were shot. When we dragged him out of the water, fat black leeches covered his body.

I had seen leeches before, but not this many or this big. Soon most of the other men were coming out of the river with these disgusting parasites all over them. It took a while for us to burn them off with cigarettes. After that, we still bathed in the rivers and streams but were much more careful. The corpsmen carried acid to burn off the leeches.

After about a month, the Seabees[7] drilled a well and set up showers for us. Those showers were great, after the leeches.

---

6 LSD – Landing Ship Dock
7 For CBs – Construction Batallion

Becoming a Marine

We boarded the plane in Oklahoma City. It was my first plane ride. In Dallas, we changed to a jet and flew non-stop to San Diego. We arrived at about nine o'clock on June 6, 1963. The buses came one at a time to pick up the Army, Navy and Air Force recruits, but no bus for the Marines. The guy in charge of our four-man group called the Marine Corps Recruit Depot to check in and request transportation. An hour later, he called again – and after another hour, he called once more. Nothing.

About two o'clock in the morning, a six-ton truck pulled up. A Marine sergeant jumped out yelling at the top of his voice, "Everybody who is going to the Marine Recruit Depot get over here. If you have chewing gum or cigarettes, get rid of them now. Get in the truck. Sit down and shut up. Move it. Move it."

Bouncing over ruts, skidding around curves, the ride to the recruit depot in the middle of the night was wild. We sat in the back of the truck in shock, afraid to speak. Our Marine Corps training had just begun.

When we arrived at the recruit depot, the sergeant shouted, "Get out of the truck, you maggots". He pointed at some yellow footprints. "Get on those foot prints. Stand at attention. Look straight ahead. Don't you eyeball me, you piece of scum." (This is the G rated version).

From there we marched to a building where they issued us a bucket[8] and uniforms. Then they took us to the barbershop. As the barber prepared to cut off the beautiful locks I was so proud of he asked, "Son, do you want to keep these curls?"

"Yes Sir," I replied.

"Okay," he said. "Hold out your hands, they're falling."

After the barbershop, we hit the shower. Now it was about 4:30 A.M. and time for bed. The sergeant marched us into a room and shouted, "Hit the rack, girls."

Of course, we were too slow and too noisy. He made us get in the rack and then get out of the rack. This went on for about twenty minutes. Finally, he turned out the lights and left the room. Just as I closed my eyes and whispered, **"Oh God, what have I done?"** the lights came on and a trashcan rolled down the aisle. The sergeant bellowed, "Reveille! Hit the deck, you maggots. You have two minutes to get dressed and be standing at attention outside."

The first day was the worst day of training for me. Except for Charlie Sides, I did not know any of the bareheaded recruits around me. Everything was new and confusing. Exhausted, we stumbled from one activity to the next. We were assigned to Platoon 237. Staff Sergeant Foster was our platoon commander. That night, we fell onto our bunks and drifted off to

---

8   We used the bucket to carry stuff and to sit on during training.

sleep listening to the drill instructor playing Bobby Bare's *Detroit City*. "I want to go home, I want to go home. Oh how I want to go home." Whenever I hear that song now, I think of boot camp.

From there the training became more physical - and I loved it. This was the challenge I had been looking for. On the runs, I was always at the front of the platoon - that is, until my fellow "Okie" and friend, Charlie Sides, began to fall out. He was a city boy – tall and slim – unused to this kind of punishment. I would go back and get him, carry his gear and sometimes him. "We're from Oklahoma. We can't let these other guys beat us," we'd say to each other when the going got tough. "Let's show them what we are made of." Charlie wanted to be a Marine more than anything. So did I. In the end, we were proud to be in the Regimental Honor Platoon.

Basic training took four months. Then we took a fourteen-day leave. We were in the staging battalion at Camp Pendleton waiting to be shipped to Hawaii to join Delta Company, 1st Battalion, 4th Marines, 1st Marine Brigade, FMF when President Kennedy was assassinated in Dallas. All liberty was canceled and we were put on stand by.

Suddenly, what it meant to be a Marine took on a different meaning. I'd grown up during the Cold War. China and the Soviet Union had the bomb. The communist threat seemed very real when Fidel Castro took over in Cuba only ninety miles from Key West, Florida. Some of the people around me had narrowly avoided participation in the Bay of Pigs in 1961. In the fall of 1962, the Cuban Missile Crisis set everyone's nerves jangling again. Naturally, the country suspected

Cuba had a part in the assassination. Although I still had a lot of training in front of me, I was prepared to do whatever it was that my country asked of me.

When Lee Harvey Oswald was arrested and it became clear that we wouldn't be attacking Cuba, our attention turned back to the next part of our training.

While we were at Camp Pendleton, Charlie received orders to report to a different battalion. We'd grown close over the past months and I was sorry that we wouldn't serve together in the same group. Although I hoped that our paths would cross in the future, I never saw him again.

In December, we boarded the U.S.S. General Mann on our way to Hawaii. On the third day out of San Diego, the ship began to take on water. I was a good swimmer, but land was a long way away by then. I was a country boy from the middle of the continent. Going fishing on a pond in a leaky rowboat was my only comparable experience and I always came home from those adventures with wet feet. Having no concept of the giant on-board pumps that can process a bazillion gallons a minute, I was nervous. However, to my great relief, the sailors solved the problem and we proceeded with no further incidents.

You have to give the Navy credit. They provide good transportation for the Marines. We Marines depend on them a lot while we are learning to walk on water.

On December 6, we landed at Pearl Harbor. From there we were bused to Kaneohe Bay Marine Corps Air Station where Delta Company, 1st Battalion, 4th Marines, 1st Marine Brigade, FMF was stationed. To be a U.S. Marine and live in paradise - how lucky could a seventeen-year-old farm boy get? "God must be smiling on me," I thought as I looked around.

I was assigned to 2nd Platoon of Delta Company 1/4[9] and the paradise concept shattered. Hawaii provided a wide range of training from guerrilla, jungle and urban warfare to cold weather training on the mountain peaks of Mauna Loa on the Big Island. Our Battalion Commander, Col. A. I. Thomas, believed in using them all, and often. The other battalions referred to us as A. I.'s roadrunners. After training exercises, the other battalions called for trucks to take them back to the staging areas. We walked.

All the things the Navy Seals and the Army Special Forces brag about were just a way of life for the average 1/4 grunt. Then there were times we trained hard. We made beach landings in Amtracks and in Mike boats[10]. We repelled out of choppers fifty feet above the surface and emerged from submarines fifty feet below the surface. We practiced fighting with rifles, knives and hand-to-hand. We learned to work with tanks, rockets, artillery and close air support. We studied bio-chemical warfare. We drilled in escape and evasion and survival techniques.[11] I loved being a part of this tough, well-trained, enthusiastic team.

9 The 1st Battalion, 4th Marines is commonly referred to as "1/4".
10 A Mike boat is an open boat with a flat bottom and a ramp in the front that drops down to let you out. We were loaded into them down the side of a ship using cargo nets.

In early 1964, 1/4 participated in war games in Taiwan. We were the aggressor force against the 3rd Marine Division from Camp Pendleton in a three week exercise. We arrived in Taiwan a month early to prepare.

A platoon of Chinese Marines attached to 2nd Platoon was supposed to stay with us throughout the exercise. At the end of the first day, they pulled out saying that we were too crazy. As the exercise began, we were to hit Division as they came ashore and then pull back to our position in the mountain jungles. Division came ashore very confident - yelling obscenities as to where they were going to shove our surfboards.

Soon cries of "Corpsman up" replaced those obscenities as they reached the first hill and the sharp needles of huge hemp plants. We pulled back. Our strategy was to take out command and control rather than taking the infantry units head on - although Corporal Kellogg from 1st Platoon did capture a platoon by himself[12].

On the fourteenth day, the 2nd Platoon, under the command of 1st Lieutenant Dawson, made a surprise raid on one of the Regimental Command Posts and captured the Regimental Commander. At the same

---

11 It was during this time that the U.S. Army had a program called Operation SHAD where they secretly subjected Marines and sailors of the 1st Marine Brigade and the ships of the 7th Fleet to biochemical agents. This was between the years of 1963 to 1965. This is classified information so we have not been able to discover how many men and what units were involved.

12 Gunnery Sergeant Kellogg later received the Medal of Honor for his service in Vietnam.

time, other units seized the other commanders including Division - and Division surrendered. We secured the exercise and received a few days of liberty in Japan.

During this time, I stood duty as Corporal of the Guard aboard ship, which was a unique experience. We had three prisoners on bread and water. The brig was down in the bow of the ship with no lights. One thing for sure, I did not want to be in the brig on a ship!

Back in Hawaii during May of 1964, Lieutenant Dawson left us and Lieutenant James M. Mitchell, Jr. became our Platoon Commander. As we stood in formation, the company commander introduced Lieutenant Mitchell to us. We mumbled among ourselves, "What in the world is this"? The lieutenant was only about 5' 5" tall! A Marine that short was rare in those days. We soon learned that his height had nothing to do with the man that he was. In the months ahead, he became the most respected and admired officer in the battalion. I was further impressed when I learned that he went to college on a *basketball* scholarship.

Lieutenant Mitchell inspired our platoon to excel in everything we did. He entered us in the Marine Corps Top Squad competition. We made it to the finals to represent the 1st Marine Brigade at Quantico. We were well ahead of our competition when our squad leader passed out from dehydration. We had to carry him to a certain point before we could get a replacement. By the time we brought in another squad leader, we had fallen behind. As the finish line drew near, we were gaining fast but not fast enough. We lost that competition, but we knew in our hearts and minds that under the leadership of 1st Lieutenant James M. Mitchell, Jr., 2nd Platoon Delta Company 1st Battalion 4th Marines 1st Marine Brigade FMF was without a doubt one of the best platoons in the United States Marine Corps.

Life in Hawaii was good. Training filled our days but evenings and weekends were free. I made many good friends there - Norm Kegerreis and Ed Paulus to name two. Everyone called Ed Paulus, "Eddie G". He went through boot camp at Parris Island. Because I took my training in San Diego, he called me a "Hollywood Marine". He still does. In return, I tease him about classes we took on the care and nomenclature of Marine Corps sunglasses.

Lieutenant Mitchell encouraged us to continue our education, especially those of us who had not finished high school. He made it possible for us to take night classes through USAFI[13] and when we were ready, he arranged for a group to take the GED test. I passed both the high school and first year of college test. My self-confidence soared.

On the weekends, a group of 1/4 Marines participated in cross-country running tournaments which included everything from a one-mile jog to a full marathon. These Marines held the island records for the one-mile, two-mile and marathon events. I was pleased when the group invited me to join them. One of the runners was a 1st Lieutenant whose name I don't remember. The leadership and coaching roles fell to him. He went to Brigade, asked for, and received official sanctions to form the Hawaiian Marine Cross Country Track Team. Two weeks of extensive training and tryouts followed. I was determined to make the cut. Amused by the intensity of my efforts, my friend, Eddie G, gave me the name "Guts and Hack It". At the end of tryouts, I made the team. A schedule was set to run at several major universities back in the "world". Triumphant, I turned, looked across the ocean and shouted, "Look at me now, Coach!"

In early 1965, 1/4 was once again chosen to participate in war games as the aggressor force against the 3rd Division, in Operation Silver Lance - this time at Camp Pendleton, California. After the operation, 1/4 would stay to field test a new rifle the US military was considering, the AR15. However, that would not happen as the situation in Vietnam began heating up and the 4th Marines left Hawaii for South East Asia. Consequently, the military issued the AR15 for combat use before it was properly tested. Many lives were lost

---

13 USAFI - United States Armed Forces Institute

because of problems with that rifle. The designers eventually reworked it and it evolved into what would become the M16. In my opinion, neither weapon rivaled the old M14s. It was like Southwestern Bell. You could reach out and touch someone – long-distance.

In March 1965, the 4th Marines went to Okinawa where the 1st Battalion began Raider School. In April, 3/4 went to Vietnam. As it became more apparent that we were about to ship out[14], our command began a ritual of "mount out" inspections. This included packing everything we had in two sea bags. In one, we packed the things we wanted to leave behind. In the other sea bag, we stowed everything we would take with us. Then we took it along with all our combat gear and marched to a field where we waited for trucks to take us to Pearl Harbor to board the ship. On practice runs, we returned to the barracks and stood a "junk on the bunk" inspection where we placed everything from both sea bags in a specific manner on our bunks, in our wall locker and in our footlockers. Then we put everything away.

At first, we were required to have everything ready and waiting for the trucks in four hours, then later in two hours. After a couple of weeks of "mount out" inspections anytime day or night, week days and weekends, total frustration set in.

To our great surprise, we got some good news. Get everything in the two sea bags, they told us. Stage[15] the

---

14 Today they call it being "deployed". In those days, Marines were transported mostly by ship.

15 Place into storage.

one. Take the other. Fall out in the field. When it was over, we would take everything back to the barracks, put it away and then go on liberty. In our excitement, we decided to skip a few steps in the process. We stuffed our pillows in the one sea bag and fell out in the field. To our great surprise, this was the one time the IG[16], General Victor Krulak, inspected our sea bags. You guessed it. That was one unhappy little general screaming, "What are you going to do, beat the enemy to death with your pillows?"

There was no liberty that day.

A few days later, it was the real thing. We went to Okinawa to begin Raider training. We were excited. This would be a real feather in our caps. Raiders were the "baddest" of the bad, toughest of the tough. We would be the first Marine Raider Battalion since the Korean Conflict. However, the Vietnam War cut our training short.

We boarded the U.S.S. Johnston en route to Chu Lai, South Vietnam.

A couple of days before we reached our debarkation point the word came down, "Beesley, the Lieutenant wants to see you."

Eager to please, I hustled to see what was up.

The Lieutenant asked, "How would you feel about becoming a squad leader?"

I was shocked. Usually squad leaders are sergeants, E-5s, sometimes corporals, E-4s, but I was a Lance

---

16 IG -– Inspector General

Corporal, E-3 and only nineteen years old. Up to this point, I had been a grenadier[17] and had not even been a fire team leader. In two days, we would be making a beach landing in an area where Reconnaissance reported eight battalions of hardcore VC[18].

I swallowed my pride and answered, "Sir, I am just a kid. I'm not sure I'm mature enough to take the responsibility of the whole squad. Surely, you could find a sergeant somewhere." Not wanting to seem ungrateful, I added, "If you can't, you are my leader and I will do whatever you ask me to."

The next day the Lieutenant called me in again. He had found a sergeant in supply.

I turned in my M79 grenade launcher and my .45 sidearm in exchange for a M14 rifle and became a fire team leader.

It was to be a momentous decision for all of us.

---

17 Marine who carries the grenade launcher.

18 VC –- Viet Cong

THE CALL OF THE WALL -- August 31, 1995

I'm not bad, but the bad call me 'boss'.

I wake up first. Dillon snuggles close to me. Connie stays in bed to allow me to get up and be alone with my thoughts for a while. Although she doesn't completely understand what is going on inside my head, she knows this is a major event in my life and she is very understanding. I love her so much.

I get in the bathtub. The water is so hot that my skin turns red. It feels good. I could almost go to sleep except for the thoughts racing through my mind - thoughts of rice paddies, jungles - patrols that lasted for days at a time. No showers, no bathtubs - nothing except rivers and streams filled with huge blood-sucking leeches. Turning our socks and skivvies inside out on alternate days - trying to avoid jungle rot, or the creeping crud, as we called it.

The Wall is calling me. I remember the poor farm boy growing up in rural Oklahoma - the wheelchair athlete, the double amputee who would become a successful businessman against all the odds, a good father, husband, grandfather. Yes, they are all with me - but today I have a meeting with that gung ho young Marine Corporal who has been wandering so hopelessly lost for these past thirty years. **God, I miss him.**

I must get moving. The dress blues given to me by my friends, Danny and Christy Snellgroves, are waiting[19]. This is the first time I will wear a complete dress blue uniform. We stop at Bob Evans for breakfast. I am so proud that I don't know how to keep the buttons on my blouse from popping off. Everyone notices us but no one asks. I guess they know there is something very special happening today.

Dillon insists on sitting beside me. It makes his grandmother nervous. She is afraid he will get the Blues dirty. He is only four years old but he seems to understand what is happening. He is a handsome young man. Connie sits across the table wearing a

19 We met Christy during Desert Storm, the first Iraq war. Her husband, Danny, was a Marine with the reserve unit in Broken Arrow, Oklahoma, and was deployed to Kuwait. Connie and I were helping with the support group. Connie wrote to Danny while he was in Kuwait. We met him when he returned home. They became very good friends of ours.

pretty dress. She is a wonderful wife. Who would have thought thirty years ago that I would end up married to a grandma? I love it.

With breakfast finished, we begin the last leg of the trip. As we drive through Washington D. C., we stop at a light. A man in his late twenties walks up to the car with a squeegee. I wave him away. He makes some kind of remark as he walks toward the car behind me. I respond sarcastically, "Get a job."

Connie says, "Honey, you don't know unless you have walked in his shoes."

I reply, "I know about being poor. I have been there".

As the light changes and we continue on our way, we discuss the incident. I concede Connie is right. That is why I wear this uniform so that Americans can be free to do what they will, want to, or must.

We drive on. Dillon is now sitting on Grandma's lap. She points out things to him. I try to be part of the conversation but my mind is churning as we draw nearer to the Wall. I am nervous. I slow down to postpone this event, but the force pulls me onward.

Vietnam

On May 7, 1965 at 8:00 A.M., we headed toward the beach at Chu Lai via Amtracks. Tension mounted. I recalled that the average life expectancy of a Marine rifleman on a beach landing was forty-five seconds. It was a sobering thought, but I was ready.

However, instead of opposing enemy forces, a large banner stating the "Vietnamese People Welcome 1/4" greeted us. A group of U.S. Army advisers, in an attempt to take a slap at the Marines, made a little sign that said, "Welcome Marines, the U.S. Army is here and the situation is well in hand." That just shows you how wrong the Army got it AGAIN.

Chu Lai was a flat plain, serviced by a major road and close to the coast so we could get to it from the sea. The whole time I was in Vietnam, I don't remember visiting a ville or hamlet called Chu Lai. I later found out that when General Krulak chose the area for an airstrip, it had no official name. There wasn't much there, so he used the Mandarin Chinese characters for his own name to christen it "Chu Lai".

The first three days we set up a roadblock on Highway 1 with very little opposition. Then we pulled back and set up a perimeter around an area where the Seabees would build the airstrip envisaged by General Krulak. Running parallel to the beach, the field would be two to three thousand feet long and seventy-two feet wide. With its parallel taxiways, refueling facilities and maintenance areas, the facility was almost like an aircraft-carrier deck built on shore. It was even equipped with arresting gear so the aircraft could use their tail hooks for very short field landings. The Seabees worked fast. Twenty-six days in country, we landed our first jet.

Shortly after we dug in, we took our first casualty to friendly fire. A friend from another platoon who had come over to visit, accidentally shot Lance Corporal Brickie Bowman through the neck with a tracer round. They got Brickie on a chopper but he never made it to the hospital on board the U.S.S. Iwo Jima, sitting out in the South China Sea for support.

A few days later on the other side of the line, another Lance Corporal received a "Dear John" letter and took his own life with his .45.

We were Marines but we were also kids. I was nineteen. My friend, Eddie G, was a little older. The Lieutenant was twenty-five. Up to that point, we felt invulnerable. The loss left us shocked and horrified.

Things were tense. We were still waiting for those eight battalions of Viet Cong. It was bad news for some of the local farmers when their pigs tripped illumination grenades we had placed in front of our positions. Can you say "dead meat"? Or "Oh my achin bacon"?

We went in believing that we were there to help the South Vietnamese people but it didn't take long for us to realize that they just wanted to harvest their rice and would rather that we leave. Regardless, we had an obligation to them based on existing treaties. We were there to stay for a while.

Life for a 1/4 grunt in Vietnam was little different from that experienced by earlier Jarheads[20] in a battle zone. It was like camping out in places where other folks shot at you from time to time. When we landed, we were prepared to survive for thirty-days without additional supplies. In our sea bags, we had three changes of clothing and an extra pair of boots. We seldom had a chance to wash our clothes. When the stink got too bad, we turned them inside out.

In the beginning, every Marine packed a shelter-half on his back. It had snaps so that two together created a pup tent where we slept when not in our fighting holes. After we'd been there awhile, we got a tent big enough for eight men and rested on what we called rubber ladies - blow up air mattresses. We averaged three or four hours of sleep a night so when we slept, we slept soundly. The first night we had a big rain after the rubber ladies arrived was a real gully-washer. When we woke up, we were all in a pile because the mattresses floated and the water carried us down to one end of the tent.

We ate C-Rations - canned food packed so that there was a meal for one person in a box. It included some protein, vegetable, starch and dessert. There were several varieties like pressed ham, turkey, and ham and lima beans. We warmed up our food with little bars that gave off heat, but sometimes while on patrol we didn't have any. When eaten cold, the ham and lima beans was about the nastiest stuff I ever tasted.

Rations included a tiny pack of cigarettes left over from World War II. They were old and dry but we

---

20 Marines are called "Jarheads" because they were the first group to carry individual rations into the field packed into little jars.

smoked them anyway. Sometimes they gave us beer. It was bad too, but after we'd been there awhile, we were glad to get it.

When we were supplied, we got three boxes a day – on patrol, only one. Sure, we were hungrier some days than others, but Marines don't whine. We sucked it up and went about our business – even when all we had to eat was ham and lima beans.

Vietnam was hot and we were doing a lot of physical labor. We were always thirsty so we took twelve salt tablets a day and drank lots of water. While in camp, we had water buffalos,[21] but on patrol we had to fill our canteens from the streams and rivers. We carried water purification tablets to clean it up for drinking.

We guarded an area up to twenty miles from our base camp to insure that Charlie[22] didn't move in too close to the airstrip. We ran day patrols, night patrols, platoon patrols, company patrols. Choppers dropped us out on peninsulas where we'd go on search-and-destroy missions. We would take a hill one day and give it back the next.

The area around Chu Lai was beautiful but deadly. The beach was a thick layer of loose golden sand. It was a backbreaking job to move heavy equipment across it. The landscape ranged from grassy plains to rice paddies to open areas criss-crossed with hedgerows to thick jungle. The enemy used this diversity to their

_____

21 Water tanks

22 Slang for Viet Cong – VC, Victor Charlie.

advantage by planting booby traps where we were most likely to walk or fall or jump behind vegetation during firefights.

My sense of direction never let me down. Once we were on a night mission to rendezvous with a platoon from Bravo Company. The brush got thicker and thicker, slowing our progress. We came to a stop. I sighed and looked up. The canopy was so dense that I couldn't see the stars. I bet myself that we were lost.

Sure enough, after a few minutes, the Lieutenant called me up to the front of the line. The group on point got turned around in the darkness and we were nowhere near where we were supposed to be.

At the Lieutenant's request, I got my bearings and took over the point position. The jungle was so dense that I had to hack the foliage out of our way. Before long, we reached a solid wall of vines. I realized that there had to be another way so I climbed up to see if I could find another route out. The vegetation was so thick that we could walk across it for several hundred feet before climbing back down.

When we reached our rendezvous point, the other platoon had already come and gone.

After a month of bathing in leech-infested streams, we were delighted when the Seabees dug a well and set up a shower for us. My friend, Norm Kegerreis, was with the first group heading down to test the new facilities. The guys were clowning around having a good time as they climbed into the truck. A grenade fell out of someone's grenade pouch and the pin popped loose. The explosion caused other grenades to detonate. A five-gallon gas can strapped on the back of the truck cab exploded into a ball of fire. Norm remembers seeing people across from him going up in the air in slow motion. One kid landed in Norm's lap - horribly mutilated by the blast – then slid onto the floor of the truck and died. Several Marines were killed and several more were wounded. Somehow, Norm was spared.

Eager for a break from the endless patrols, I was excited when the prospect of R&R[23] in Bangkok arose and disappointed when I couldn't go. When the plane crashed killing all on board, I was both relieved and troubled. I had never seen death before - not like this - not like in Vietnam. I began to pull into my bubble of security. If I didn't know the people around me that well, then when they were gone, they were just gone. If you get too personal, you lose your mind. I kept shoving it back. The duty thing kicked in. My job became my Number One focus. The Army plans an avenue of retreat, but with the Marines, there is no retreat. You achieve the objective or you are dead. "Suck it up, Marine. Keep going." With that mindset, when friends drop, it hurts but you go on - and we did. I did.

Then we began to get news that our countrymen were turning against the war and thousands were marching in mass demonstrations. Hanoi Hannah informed us that our girlfriends were going out with other guys. Boy did she get that right!

We were in a hopeless situation. It seemed like our fellow citizens had turned their hate for war into hate for those of us in the military. On top of that, it was

---

23 R&R -– Rest and Recuperation

impossible to understand some of our orders. We were bigger, stronger, badder than the other side. Our resources were endless - but the rules changed. We couldn't carry loaded rifles anymore, then we couldn't fire until the enemy shot at us. It became painfully clear that our government was not going to let us win this war. We became frustrated and angry. The best we could hope for was to survive until our time was up and we could go home - and home was beginning to seem a long way away. The Animals' anthem, "We Gotta Get Out of This Place", became the Vietnam grunt's theme song. Marines who had been in country more than a few weeks had a look of hopelessness in their eyes. We called it the "thousand yard stare".

As we lost Marines, we replaced them with kids straight out of boot camp, many of them only seventeen years old. Somehow, the young ones were always assigned to my fire team. The other fire teams in the squad had two young men each. My team had six sometimes seven. At nineteen, I was the old man - the one with experience - the one others relied on. I accepted the responsibility but it weighed on me. Many nights as I stood watch to let my men get some much-needed rest, I looked toward the stars with tears streaming down my face and whispered, **"Please God, help me get these kids home safe."**

Often while the other platoon leaders were sleeping, Lieutenant Mitchell came around to check the line. He would sit and talk with me about my plans for the future and about my family. He also talked about the baby he and his wife, Jan, were expecting. He made me feel useful - important - like my contributions counted. He made me think he trusted my judgment - that he trusted me.

34

This personal contact made me realize what a great leader he was. I tried my best to follow his example and share a little bit of myself with others too. I wanted out of Vietnam but I was still a Marine. The Corps was my life. I thought about maybe becoming a drill instructor when I rotated back to the real world.

My friend, Norm Kegerreis, and I were both promoted to Corporal around the same time. Usually there weren't two corporals in one squad so Sergeant Belcher, our squad leader, decided to transfer one of us to another unit. Both of us wanted to go. I had seniority[24] and thought I should be the one reassigned. Norm remembers that the Lieutenant had us draw straws and he won. I just remember that the Lieutenant kept me for some reason and Norm moved on. I was disappointed, but I sucked it up and kept on trying to do the best job possible under the circumstances.

At full strength, a platoon should have forty-seven men. We had twenty-one to twenty-six at a time. Lieutenant Mitchell was the commander. Staff Sergeant Sam Fernandez was the platoon sergeant. Under him were four squads led by Sergeant Bolt, Corporal McHenry, Corporal Paulus (my friend Eddie G) and Sergeant Belcher. The fire team is the smallest organizational unit. Normally it has four people – the Team Leader, an automatic rifleman and two riflemen.

---

24 Seniority is a big thing in the Marines. Story: Two guys go into a tavern. The recruiter comes in, says, "I'll give you two free beers if you join the Corps." The first guy takes the deal and sits down at a table in the corner. The recruiter says to the next guy, "I'll give you a free beer if you join the Corps." The second man agrees and sits down next to the first one and says, "Hey man, did you see that, a free beer just for joining the Corps." "That's nothing," the first man says, "in the OLD Corps, they gave us two."

I was the Fire Team Leader under Sergeant Belcher and since I had the most men, we were the main group.

Despite the usual tradition and the big to-do with Norm Kegerreis, Corporal Daniel Duffy was a member of my team even though he outranked me. I didn't know him well, but I know he liked being a Marine. Others on my team included L/Cpl[25] Proctor, PFC[26] Burns, PFC Bailey, PFC Foster and PFC Cobb.

Toward the end of July, the Lieutenant got word that he had a baby girl. Cheers went up through the whole platoon. It was as if she was "our" baby girl. We'd been in Nam three months, but there had been so much death and ugliness. That little girl gave me hope that it would be over someday and I'd be able to go home and be with my own family again. I smiled as the Lieutenant shared his pictures of Jan and little Erin with us. He was so proud.

---

25 L/Cpl –- Lance Corporal

26 PFC –- Private First Class

THE CALL OF THE WALL

To Boldly Go Where A FEW GOOD MEN Have Gone Before

We find a parking place. There is a very large crowd today. We get out of the car and make our way toward the Wall. We round the corner at the Lincoln Monument and I see the American flag flying high. My heart skips a beat or two. Goose bumps cover my body. Anxiety grips me. We cross the street and continue toward the Wall. When we reach the flagpole, I see the Wall in the distance. For a moment, I sit frozen as I experience every emotion I have ever known.

I am brought back to reality as Dillon, pointing to a bronze statue of three soldiers that represent the men who fought in Vietnam, says "Pa, tell me about these boys."

I tell him about the clothes, boots, weapons, etc. When I finish, he says, "Say it again Pa."

As I began again, a crowd gathers around, watching Dillon and me. A group of Japanese tourists asks if they can take pictures. A little red haired boy has been listening. He asks me to tell him about the soldiers. I am happy to keep talking. It gives me more time to prepare myself to face the Wall. After telling about "the boys" four or five times, I gather myself together. Turning toward the Wall, I push my chair slowly in that direction.

The crowd files past. I watch them while trying to determine in my own mind what has brought them here. It is obvious that some are simply curious. Some are sightseeing. Some are those "touchy, feely" people who want to make themselves feel good about building a monument to those who they had cursed and spit on and protested.[27]

A mother and father are crying, praying -- and trying to comfort one another as they find the name of their son. Lying against the Wall, I see a picture of three children with a letter attached. It reads, "We never met you, but we love you Uncle Bobby".

---

27 The "Wall" was not built by a grateful nation, but by Vietnam Veterans themselves.

August 30 - 31, 1965

In mid-August, the Marines participated in the Battle of Chu Lai – code name Operation Starlight.[28] It was the first major battle in Vietnam. We had been in country three months at that point. A VC deserter revealed that the headquarters for the 1st Viet Cong Regiment was twelve miles south of Chu Lai. He indicated that about fifteen hundred VC troops were ready to attack the Chu Lai airfield and the surrounding Marine positions.

A preemptive attack against the Viet Cong by 2/4, 3/3 and 3/7 Marines ended on August 24. We were in reserve protecting the Chu Lai airfield during that time. Six hundred and thirteen Viet Cong were killed at a cost of fifty-one Marines killed and two hundred and three wounded.

Something was up. The evening of August 30, the Company Commander called Lieutenant Mitchell to the Command Post to be briefed on the patrol assigned to the 2nd Platoon for the next day. Then the Lieutenant called the squad leaders together to brief them. The squad leaders in turn called the fire team leaders to explain the details of the mission.

Our squad leader, Sergeant Belcher, looked at me and said, "Beesley, you will take point."

28 The first two Medals of Honor of the Vietnam War were given for action in this battle.

"No problem," I said, "we can do that."

"No I don't mean your team, I mean you".

On several other occasions while on night patrols, Lieutenant Mitchell had called me up to take point and get us to our destination. As a boy down on the farm, I did a lot of hunting at night and had a natural sense of direction. Usually, I didn't mind.

Somehow, this time it seemed all wrong.

On a patrol earlier that day, I had stepped in a hole. A punji stake[29] went through my boot and stuck into the inside of my left ankle. I did not tell anyone. About a month before, a couple of our guys tripped a booby trap and received the Purple Heart for some pea to marble size shrapnel wounds. Some thought that it was not appropriate to get a Purple Heart for such an insignificant injury. There was something un-Marine-like about it.

No one ever knew about my wound, but maybe it had something to do with my attitude that night. I told Sergeant Belcher that I would not take point anymore. I explained that I was a Corporal[30] and it was not in my job description. I was going home in just over a month and had a short-timer's attitude about taking undue chances. Even so, I was a stand-up Marine – used to taking orders. It was the first time that I questioned what I was being asked to do.

---

29 A punji stake is a piece of bamboo sharpened and covered with human waste in order to cause almost instant infection.

30 I had been promoted to Corporal with the highest cutting score in the Battalion.

After a heated argument, Sergeant Belcher called in Staff Sergeant Fernandez to settle the dispute. Staff Sergeant Fernandez informed me that this was a very important patrol and that Lieutenant Mitchell had told Sergeant Belcher to put me on point. That information took the wind out of my sails. If the Lieutenant wanted me on point, there must be a reason.

We agreed that I would be point man but that it was the last time anyone would ask me to do it.

Around 8:00 A.M. the next day, the whole platoon saddled up and headed north. I was on point. Proctor followed - then Burns, Foster, Cobb and Duffy. Bailey would not be going with us today. He was at company headquarters for office hours. Sergeant Belcher, the Lieutenant and the two corpsmen were behind Duffy. Eddie G's squad was on the right flank, McHenry's squad on the left. Sergeant Bolt's squad brought up the rear. As we moved north, we crossed a ravine. Proctor jumped in and injured both of his ankles. We had to call for the choppers to evacuate him.

Around 9:30 A.M. it was approaching 110 degrees Fahrenheit. We continued across an open field to the northwest making no effort to conceal our advance. After a bit, we came to a hedgerow. The hedge was about ten to twelve feet tall. As I stepped through an opening in the hedge, I spotted a land mine lying on the ground beside a hole. Apparently, we had come upon someone planting the mine and they'd left in a hurry.

I held up the patrol and called for the Lieutenant to come up and decide what we should do. Should we dig our way through the minefield, back out and blow it or what? As I waited, Lieutenant Mitchell and Corporal

Duffy arced around behind me and pushed through the hedge to the front and left of me. They came out pretty much where the mine lay on the trail.

Sergeant Bolt hustled up from the rear and came through the same opening I'd found. As Bolt squeezed past on the trail, he brushed against me and I took one step back. As I did, I looked down to see where to set my foot.

To my horror, I saw a different mine[31] come up out of the ground between my feet.

The explosion was tremendous.

The force threw me up and back over the twelve-foot hedge into the opening. I landed on my back. I thought that my head had exploded from the concussion. Instinctively I grabbed it with both hands expecting to find part of it missing. It was still there.

I'M STILL ALIVE, I thought but my relief was short-lived.

I looked down toward my feet. My right trouser leg was tattered with my blousing garter[32] hanging from it.

Weird. I squinted, trying to figure it out.

At that instant, the pain hit. It felt as if my legs were on fire.

---

31 Bouncing Betty land mine used by VC/NVA—when a trip wire or pressure fuse is hit, a projectile bounds three feet upward and explodes with a fifty foot casualty radius.

32 Boot band

42

In the distance, I heard the Lieutenant yelling for the squad leaders to set up a perimeter and call for the choppers.

I looked down and saw that both trouser legs were tattered and torn - and there were jagged bones with no flesh on them sticking out where my feet used to be.

The smell of gunpowder, the burning flesh, the scorching heat, the pain, dust and smoke, blood and torn flesh everywhere - I AM DYING! I don't want to die! I am not ready to die!

I was losing it - going into shock.

I tried to remember the 23rd Psalm, but I couldn't put the words together in sequence. I gave up in frustration and panic overwhelmed me.

GOD, PLEASE DON'T LET ME DIE IN THIS AWFUL PLACE. As if dying somewhere else would make me less dead.

I knew I needed to calm down - regain control. Focus.

Deep down inside me, a voice said, **"SUCK IT UP, MARINE. This is what it's all about - to do or die. It's gut-check time."**

My mind cleared for a moment and my training came back. I had to stop the bleeding. I fumbled for my first aid kit. I found the compression bandage and opened it but I was too weak to do more. I had already lost too much blood.

Our young corpsman yelled at me - something about a belt. I looked down. I was not wearing one.

He took his own belt and one from someone else to make tourniquets for my legs.

"Give me something for the pain," I begged him.

"I already did," he said and moved on to someone else.

The senior corpsman, Staff Sergeant Fernandez and Sergeant Belcher ran to the Lieutenant and Corporal Duffy on the other side of the hedgerow.

I heard someone screaming, "He's dying, he's dying."

Another voice yelled, "Knock him out!"

The screaming stopped.[33]

From his position on the right flank, Eddie G found me. I could hear the anguish in his voice as he yelled, "JESUS #$#^% CHRIST where are those ^%$#% choppers?"

I felt myself drifting away. Everything closed in around me. I knew I was dying.

NO.

---

33 When the older corpsman saw the carnage and devastation, he freaked. Staff Sergeant Fernandez ordered Sergeant Belcher to knock him out. Sergeant Belcher hit the corpsman with the butt of his shotgun and knocked him out.

I wouldn't die.

I focused on staying alive - but with every minute that passed, I grew weaker.

I could no longer see.

Despite the morphine the corpsman gave me, the pain was tremendous and I was tired - so tired. It would be easy to let go - but I wouldn't.

In the distance, I heard choppers coming for us - for me. It's a sound so distinct that even today it brings a tear to my eye.

Someone put me on a poncho.

Two men lifted the poncho - one at my head and one at my feet, doubling me up at the waist.

In a flash of lucidity, I saw the shredded bones of what was left of my legs - coming toward my face.

Then more darkness.

The choppers picked us up and flew back to the battalion medical station near the Chu Lai airstrip.

Somehow, I knew that either Lieutenant Mitchell or Corporal Duffy was dead. I didn't know which. I lost track of the others.

PAIN.

I was exhausted and I just didn't want to deal with it all right then. At the medical station, I pleaded with the doctor to give me something to make me sleep. He replied, "Son, if you go to sleep, you won't wake up."

While he worked on me, a corpsman pinched my cheeks to keep me awake.

I was thirsty.

Aside from my legs, it was unclear what other injuries I'd sustained so they wouldn't allow me to have water.

"I'm thirsty," I muttered.

The corpsman dipped cotton balls in water and put them in my mouth.

THE CALL OF THE WALL

If You Weren't There Then Shut Up

As I approach panel No. 2E, I see a veteran visiting the Wall for the first time. I watch his eyes scan the lines of names. He finds the one he came to see. He places both hands over his eyes. Sobbing heavily, he turns and almost runs down the walkway with his wife trying to comfort him.

My first thought is to turn around and get out of there, but I know that is not an option. I think of all the lives that changed forever because of what happened over there - names that are not on the Wall but are casualties of the Vietnam tragedy just the same. Mothers, fathers, brothers, sisters, wives, lovers, friends - and especially the children whose fathers are gone and will never come home again.

The pain in my heart is so great that I want to scream, **"God, punish those who were responsible for this."**

Just when I think I can't take it anymore, a veteran walks up and takes my hand, saying simply, "Welcome home brother." His eyes speak volumes. Spock, from Star Trek, would probably call it a mind meld as in that instant we share thoughts, feelings and emotions that only those who have been there could understand.

I suck it up.

This is not a place for anger but a place for healing.

Recovery

There were cuts on my face, bumps on my head and a large piece of shrapnel embedded in my side. All I knew was that my legs were gone - and that those wounds were horrendous.

Bolt, Burns, Foster - the others injured in the blast must have been at Bmed[34] too. I don't remember them though. I didn't dare think about anyone but me. I was afraid of what would happen if my attention wavered. I knew death was but a heartbeat away. I struggled to stay awake and to endure my thirst.

What seemed like only a few minutes, a chopper carried me out to the U.S.S. Iwo Jima where they whisked me into surgery.

More pain.

More drugs.

Other wounded people lay near me. I opened my eyes. Bolt was there. He'd lost both of his legs but they were able to save one of his knees. Burns lost both feet at the ankle. He was seventeen.

More drugs. I closed my eyes and slept.

After three days, they loaded me and another wounded Marine named Joe P. Machado onto a

---

34 Bmed – Battalion Medical

chopper headed for Da Nang. I opened my eyes and saw something wet splattered over the windows just before we went down hard in enemy territory. It must have been hydraulic fluid or oil. I never knew if we were shot down or had a mechanical problem.

Eventually, an ugly angel[35] picked us up and took us on to Da Nang.

I spent three days there. The night before I left, mortar fire hit the hospital. Would this hell never end?

From Da Nang, I went to Clark Air Force Base in the Philippines for two weeks and more surgeries. I knew I was bad off but at least no one there was trying to blow me up - or shoot me down or bombard me.

After a few days, they stopped some of the medications and I began to regain my senses. When I woke up, they had a tube in my nose. It was bothering me so much that I tried to pull it out. It kept coming out like a kerchief out of a magician's sleeve. The nurses came running. The tube was in there because they'd worked on the shrapnel wound in my side. They had to put me under again to replace it.

However, I was more awake now and by the end of two weeks in the Philippines, I began to believe that I would survive. They even let me call my brother, Bill, although I don't remember much about it.

I was still on two-hour watch when they loaded me and other wounded men onto a plane for the long ride back to the States. We landed at Travis Air Force Base

---

35 Ugly angel – chopper – UH34

in California after a twenty-seven hour flight. It was not quite Oklahoma, but I was home all the same.

I remember them loading us onto a bus. Lots of other guys on stretchers like me. The route from Travis to the Oak Knoll military hospital in Oakland was known as "The Gauntlet". War protesters placed themselves strategically along the way and threw plastic bags filled with urine, human waste wrapped in tissue paper, rocks and bottles and anything else they could get their hands on - yelling obscenities, calling us "Baby Killers". Welcome home. Only in America do people have this kind of freedom.

I lived at Oak Knoll for the next eight and a half months. The complex was a group of old wooden barracks built in WWII in the foothills of east Oakland. They assigned us to wards according to our injuries or illnesses. The amputee ward was an open bay with forty-two beds, the nurses' station, a treatment room and one private room for Colonel Tunnel.

The nurses and doctors there were the best. Our surgeon's name was Salisbury. The joke was that every time one of us went to surgery, we would have "Salisbury" steak for lunch.

Even though I got double pneumonia while at Oak Knoll, I was determined to live. I was nineteen years old. In Vietnam, I was an experienced Marine. The unthinkable had happened. Now I was just a hurt kid. I'd fought off death. Life seemed especially precious. All I had to do was get well.

After more surgeries, skin grafts and time, my condition began to improve. It was a couple of months before they got me out of bed the first time. Soon I was well enough to enjoy visitors. The doctor who operated on me on the U.S.S. Iwo Jima showed up one day. He showed me photographs of what had been my legs and promised to get copies made and send them to me. He never did.

Two of my sisters brought my mother to see me. This was the first time I had seen any of my family in over two years. When I got my first liberty, we spent the weekend with my cousin who lived in the nearby city of Pittsburg. Mom and my sisters went to the exchange to buy me some clothes. As they were preparing to pay for them, mom said, "Oh, girls, we forgot to get him some socks." When she realized what she had said, she broke down and cried.

The girls thought it was funny. So did I. We laughed about it for many years.

My brother, Bill, was in the Air Force and assigned to a detail to transfer missiles between Dyess AFB in Abilene Texas and Vandenberg AFB in California. He took the opportunity to come see me. Bill and his friend from Illinois rescued me from the hospital and we spent a long weekend in a motel. They took me to some cowboy bar where Bill caused quite a commotion after he had a few too many drinks and tried to dance with some man's wife. The guy was not at all happy. He jumped up ready to fight. He was a big man - well over six feet tall and Bill's buddy was smaller, probably about five and a half feet tall. As the angry husband approached him, he looked at him and said with a drawl. "You don't want to mess with me buddy, I'm from Texas." Bill stepped between them, grabbed his friend and we made a quick exit. I still have to laugh every time I see the Texas anti-litter campaign slogan "Don't Mess with Texas."

After arriving at Oak Knoll, I learned that both Lieutenant Mitchell and Corporal Duffy had died. I'd known it was bad – but I'd hoped that at least one of them had survived. Sergeant Bolt and PFC Burns were there in the hospital with me. Our senior corpsman was also there on the psychiatric ward. He'd been in the Navy for several years, but August 31 was his first combat experience. What he'd seen that day took a terrible toll on his psyche.

Two dead. Three grievously wounded. Others less seriously hurt. I was the one on point. The one that tripped that mine. The guilt began as soon as I was conscious. I thought about August 31 a lot - wondering how what happened could have happened to me. I was experienced. I was careful. I knew that Lieutenant Mitchell wanted me up front because he trusted me. I'd done everything by the book - hadn't I?

I began to piece it together from what other people told me and from what I could remember. When D. D. Bailey[36] came to see me at Oak Knoll after he came back from Vietnam, he told me that we'd been up against an advance guard of the North Vietnamese Regular Army. So soon after Operation Starlight, maybe there was something big brewing. Maybe that's why we went out on patrol in platoon strength that day. Maybe that's why Lieutenant Mitchell wanted me on point. Unlike some of the other officers, he was cautious. He tried to

---

36 Bailey received two bronze stars in action that took place shortly after August 31, 1965.

keep us all out of harm's way whenever possible. We were used to running into the booby traps the Viet Cong left for us, but these were Bouncing Betty mines - not sharpened pieces of bamboo planted by a band of ragged saboteurs but sophisticated anti-personnel weapons setup by a well-supplied army.

The reality of my situation dawned on me and I began to think about my future. I heard that Colonel Tunnel who lost one leg below the knee was going to stay in the Marine Corps. I knew my days as a grunt were over, but I could be a Remington Raider[37]. I could type. I could file. I talked with the Colonel several times but soon learned that staying in the Corps was not an option for me.

I loved being a Marine more than anything I'd ever done in my life. Even when I was looking forward to leaving Vietnam, I never considered leaving the service. I went into the Marines to succeed. I didn't have a plan B.[38]

Up to this point, I had been a model patient - always cheerful and up beat - so much so that the head nurse appointed me Sergeant at Arms to raise the morale. Our ward was a lively place with laughing and

---

37 Remington Raider was Marine talk for office worker.

38 I had not yet learned the meaning of "Once a Marine, Always a Marine."

joking, but now the thing that gave my life meaning was being taken from me.

Things were changing all around me too. Some of the pretty nurses who had been taking care of me since I arrived at Oak Knoll left. Then, the Navy's first two male nurses began working in our ward. Being in the hospital was just not much fun any more. I began to develop an attitude. My answer to instructions and orders was, "What are they going to do, slap my hands and send me home?"

As depression began to set in I questioned, **"God, why am I still alive and the Lieutenant is dead?** He had so much to live for and I have nothing."

I could get around some, but my mental condition was bad. The doctor noticed the change in my attitude and prescribed four ounces of bourbon each night to help me sleep. The Navy issue stuff was nasty so one of the wives brought me good Kentucky Bourbon, which the hospital allowed me to keep in the drawer beside my bed. Not only did it help me make it through the nights, it helped me make it through the days.

Every day the bourbon took more control of my life.

Then God, in His infinite mercy, sent an angel to rescue me.

WESTERN UNION

CLASS OF SERVICE

This is a full-rate Telegram or Cable-gram unless its deferred character is indicated by a suitable symbol above or preceding the address.

SYMBOLS

DL = Day Letter
NL = Night Letter
LC = Deferred Cable
NLT = Cable Night Letter
Ship Radiogram

A. N. Williams, President

The filing time shown in the date line on telegrams and day letters is STANDARD TIME at point of origin. Time of receipt is STANDARD TIME at point of destination.

WA55 33 GOVT=WUX WASHINGTON DC 1 1030A

MR & MRS BEESLEY=
    BEGGS OK=

REGRET TO CONFIRM THE INJURY OF YOUR SON CORPORAL EDDIE R. BEESLEY
USMC ON 31 AUG IN THE VICINITY OF CHU LAI REPUBLIC OF VIETNAM. HE
RECEIVED TRAUMATIC AMPUTATION OF THE RIGHT LEG AT ANKLE AND LEFT
LEG AT THE KNEE FROM AN UNKNOWN EXPLOSIVE DEVICE WHILE ON PATROL.
HIS CONDITION IS CRITICAL AND PROGNOSIS GUARDED. HE IS RECEIVING
TREATMENT AT THE COMPANY "B" MEDICAL BATTALION REPUBLIC OF VIETNAM
AND FUTHER EVACUATION IS CONTEMPLATED. YOUR ANXIETY IS REALIZED
AND YOU ARE ASSURED THAT HE IS RECEIVING THE BEST OF CARE. YOU
WILL BE KEPT INFORMED OF ANY SIGNIFICANT CHANGES IN HIS CONDITION.
HIS MAILING ADDRESS REMAINS THE SAME.

    WALLACE M.GREENE,JR., GENERAL USMC, COMMANDANT USMC

WESTERN UNION

CLASS OF SERVICE

This is a full-rate Telegram or Cable-gram unless its deferred character is indicated by a suitable symbol above or preceding the address.

SYMBOLS

DL = Day Letter
NL = Night Letter
LC = Deferred Cable
NLT = Cable Night Letter
Ship Radiogram

A. N. Williams, President

The filing time shown in the date line on telegrams and day letters is STANDARD TIME at point of origin. Time of receipt is STANDARD TIME at point of destination.

WA55 33 GOVT=WUX WASHINGTON DC 4 0830A

MR & MRS HENRY BEESLEY=
    BEGGS OK=

A REPORT RECEIVED THIS HQ 3 SEPT 1966 REVEALS THAT THE CONDITION
OF YOUR SON CORPORAL EDDIE R. BEESLEY IS NOW SERIOUS BUT RECOVERY
IS EXPECTED. HE IS SCHEDULED FOR EVACUATION TO THE USAF HOSPITAL
CLARK AIR BASE PHILLIPINE ISLANDS. HE IS SCHEDULED FOR EVACUATION
TO THE US. HOWEVER THE DATE AND NAME OF THE US HOSPITAL HE WILL BE
ASSIGNED IS UNKNOWN AT THIS TIME. MAIL MAY BE ADDRESSED TO HIM AT
THE USAF HOSPITAL APO SAN FRANCISCO 9627- UNTIL HE IS EVACUATED.
YOUR ANXIETY IS REALIZED AND YOU WILL BE KEPT INFORMED OF ALL
SIGNIFICANT CHANGES IN HIS CONDITION.

    WALLACE M.GREENE,JR., GENERAL USMC, COMMANDANT USMC

THE CALL OF THE WALL

Heroes get remembered, legends live forever.

In the beginning, when people began to talk about a Vietnam War memorial, I ignored it. I was trying to forget Vietnam, not remember it. My life was full. I was busy. I didn't want to think about the Lieutenant and his family. I didn't want to think about boys dead before they were out of their teens.

Time passed and I grew stronger. I began to dream about it - a vast marble slab with fifty-eight thousand names carved on it. Somewhere on that horrific bastion were the names of people that I knew. Their faces, their voices - their laughter haunted me. I pretended not to hear, but the wall began to call me.

Today, I'm here - brushing away my reluctance - to answer that call. As the crowd separates and the cold black granite wall appears before me, I am overwhelmed. A great flood of tears pour from my eyes.

My mind fills with a dark cloud of dread. I clasp my head – paralyzed with grief. Nothing moves except the tears streaming down my cheeks and the sound of my heart beating like a bass drum in 8/8 time.

Just as I think the battle is lost, a voice deep within screams "Suck it up, Marine - and get with the program."

On that command, I regain control of my body and open my eyes.

56

There on the wall, I see them - James M. Mitchell, Jr. and Daniel Duffy.

Connie

One afternoon not long before Christmas 1965, I awoke from a bourbon-induced sleep and through bloodshot eyes saw two young ladies walk onto the ward. They were carrying magazines, candy and cookies and had come to see Freddie Bell. Freddie was a Marine from Tulsa who had lost an arm and leg from a grenade explosion. After his injury, Freddie had gone into San Francisco and was attacked by war protesters and beaten up[39]. His photo ended up in the paper.

Freddie's bed was straight across from mine. After the girls passed out the cookies and candy to everyone on the ward who wanted them, they stood by Freddie's bed talking to him. One of them was beautiful − so beautiful that everything else in the room faded away.

39 This also happened to Joe P Machado, the young man airlifted from the U.S.S. Iwo Jima to Da Nang with me back in Vietnam.

I always loved the ladies. Even as a child, I never went through that "girls are yucky" stage. However, this girl was special.

I crawled out of my bed and into my chair almost falling to the floor in my excitement. I wheeled across the isle and asked Freddie to introduce me to his friend.

He said, "This is Connie Gaudette. Connie's father is a Navy Corpsman. Connie, this is Eddie Beesley. He's from Oklahoma too."

That is all I remember from that conversation. I'm sure he introduced me to Connie's cousin, Sharon, but I don't remember.

After that, Connie and Sharon visited our ward on a regular basis bringing cookies and candy for the guys. I didn't eat sweets (real Marines don't eat pogey bait) so we never talked much, just to say "hi".

From time to time, Connie and her cousins, Sharon and Dale, would pick Freddie up and take him to dinner. They seemed to be good friends, so I played the gentleman and chose not to interfere with that relationship. I drank my bourbon and tried not to have serious thoughts about anything.

One weekend Connie called the ward to talk to Freddie. As fate would have it, Freddie was not in. She asked for some of the other guys but none of them were there. At the "end" of the list, she asked for me.

Of course, I was there. Where else would I be? I didn't have a life.

She asked if I would like to come spend the weekend at her Aunt and Uncle's home. I told her I had a problem with this because of her relationship with Freddie. She assured me that Freddie was just a friend. I told her I would like to come, but I was still not sure in my own mind if she was being straight with me about her relationship with Freddie.

When the other guys learned that she had invited me over for the weekend, they encouraged me to go. They said, "Go ahead and go, we will get you off the "hook." Freddie's prosthetic arm had a hook on it.

I spent the weekend with her and her family.

What can I say?

She fell head over heels in love with me. Six months later, we were married. After all these years, I can't remember if I was born first or married first. I think I was born married.

My last surgery was on my twentieth birthday. This time the doctors gave me a spinal block instead of putting me under anesthesia. Along with the spinal block, I had medication to make me sleep. Just as the surgeon was finishing, I began to wake up. I opened my eyes and Dr. Salisbury looked at me and said, "Oh, Beesley, it's you. If I had realized that, I would have taken your arms off while I had you here."

After surgery, Connie came to see me. A corpsmen by the name of Doc Greenough[40] pushed my bed into

_____

40 Doc Greenough would later go to FMF and be assigned to Delta 1/4 where he too would be wounded in action in Vietnam.

the screened-in porch area of the ward and put portable partitions around my bed to give us privacy.

After that surgery, the Navy concentrated on making my prostheses. This would prove to be a challenge for them as I was the first bilateral above-the-knee amputee since the Korean War. No one knew what to do with me.

They put the prostheses on me, sat me on the floor in the middle of a room and said, "Get up".

"How", I asked.

They replied, "We want you to show us".

The artificial legs had free-swinging joints for knees. At first, standing up on them seemed like an impossible task – but I was young and strong. It wasn't pretty but I did learn how to "get up".

They put me in front of a set of steps, "Climb the steps."

"How?"

"Show us"

That was the way my gait training went.

They were interested to learn from me. A young sailor had come in who lost both legs above the knee when a cable on an aircraft carrier snapped – and more were coming in from Vietnam all the time.

In the midst of this rehab phase, a nephew drowned and they gave me leave to attend his funeral.

Back in Oklahoma surrounded by family and friends, I began to feel more adventurous. I borrowed my sister's car and went out by myself. Dad got worried and sent the other boys to look for me. I was doing fine - teaching myself how to get in and out of the car, learning to walk on the prostheses. It was a matter of pride. I wanted to do things for myself - to regain my independence.

After that, I was restless when I returned to Oak Knoll. I'd had a taste of freedom and it was hard for me to get back into the routine. Emotionally, I was ready to leave and strike out on my own. After all, I had been in the hospital almost nine months.

The doctors and hospital staff would not give me any indication as to when I could go. They still had a lot to learn from me. However, the Marines had taught me to "improvise and overcome". I went to the Marine Liaison Officer and I told him I wanted to go home.

He asked me when I wanted to go.

As soon as possible, I told him, thinking maybe a few weeks or a couple of months.

To my great surprise, he answered, "How about tomorrow?"

They completed the paper work to transfer me to Treasure Island the next day. That's where the Marine Corps would officially discharge me.

The hospital staff was angry with me but that was the least of my problems. I still had to call Connie to give her the news. She was not a "happy camper". Things had happened so fast I had not had a chance to discuss my decision with her.

I arrived at Treasure Island on Friday too late to be processed that day. I had to stay through the weekend. Although Connie was angry, she picked me up and we spent the weekend at her Aunt's house.

On Monday, I was discharged and flew back to Oklahoma.

THE CALL OF THE WALL

Heaven Won't Take Us and Hell Is Afraid We'll Take Over

I stare at their names and ask myself the one question I can never answer.

Why?

Deep within the shadows of black granite, HIS face appears. The face of that young Corporal who had called me here, that part of me that I left behind on that despicable day in 1965. I realize that he can never go home again. He's destined to stand Corporal of the Guard in the shadows of this wall throughout eternity.

My heart breaks.

My mind explodes with a million memories - the beauty of the Hawaiian countryside where we trained, running in athletic competitions for the Hawaiian Marines, war games in Taiwan.

It's all I can bear.

We go back to our motel and I change out of the dress blues.

Drained, I reflect on the day as we linger over roast duck at a Chinese restaurant. I overcame so much to make this pilgrimage, yet I know there's more I must do.

I look at Connie. She and Dillon are tired, I realize - but once again, I see acceptance and understanding in her eyes.

After dinner, we drive back to the wall. It's quieter at night - more private.

I sit and think - grieve.

There are others.

I sense them in the darkness wanting to be alone with their memories.

Starting Over

The first thing on my agenda when I went back to Oklahoma was to buy a car. I found the one I wanted - a 1966 Chevelle SS 396 with a Holly 427 special carburetor. Through a friend of a friend, I found a paraplegic in Tulsa who had hand controls in his car. Together we built controls for mine.

In a couple of weeks, Connie took a vacation from her job at Pacific Bell Telephone and flew to Tulsa. Together, we drove to Fort Wayne, Indiana, to meet her family. Connie's father was on recruiting duty there at the time. We were planning to be married. I wanted to do the honorable thing and ask her father for her hand. We spent a week with her family of four brothers and two sisters. Her brother, Mike, was home on furlough after completing Army boot camp. It was an interesting week with the Marines, Navy and Army in the same house.

It was hard to find time to talk to Connie's father alone. Finally, I just asked to speak to him in private. I told him I was very much in love with his daughter and

I wanted his permission to marry her. He asked me if I was sure this was what the two of us wanted to do.

"Very sure," I said.

"Okay, you have my permission."

We drove back to Tulsa. Connie flew back to California, gave her two weeks notice then returned to Oklahoma. While she was away, I went to work for the Oklahoma State Highway Department as an engineer's aide.

When Connie returned, we stayed with my sister, Lou, and began planning our wedding. Everything was going well until Lou informed us that in less than two weeks she would be taking a family vacation. Being the honorable guy I am and not wanting to give anyone cause to say anything untoward about my bride for living with me before we were married, we decided to be married by a Justice of the Peace.

There was one glitch. I was only twenty so I asked my dad to sign for me to marry Connie. He said, "I signed for you to get your legs blowed off. I'm not signing for you to get plumb killed." Luckily, my mother agreed to sign so we could get married. Later, he warmed up to Connie and they got along great!

When we arrived at the Justice's home, there were five or six steps. I looked at Connie and jokingly said, "Honey, I don't think I can make it up those steps."

Usually when I tell this story I tell everyone she said, "I will carry you". I think what she really said was, "I'll help you".

After a weekend honeymoon, we moved into our apartment and began our life together.

It was a difficult beginning.

Like all new husbands, I had to get used to living with someone who cared about my well-being. I was getting used to many other things at the same time. I'd had some time to decompress from Vietnam while in the hospital, but the hostility I sensed from my fellow citizens toward the military bothered me. If the war was a mistake, what had my buddies died for? I pushed it back and tried not to think about it, but it passed through my mind unbidden from time to time.

I had many things I wanted to accomplish but even the simplest task was complicated now. August 31, 1965, changed my options forever. The world was not yet ready to accommodate someone with a handicap like mine. There were barriers everywhere. Life without my prostheses was impossible.

I sometimes took these frustrations out on Connie. However, my family would accept no complaints about her from me. "You be good to that little girl. You're the only family she has here," they would say.

In truth, Connie was the center of my world. Sometimes we'd play like children, tossing cold water onto each other over the shower curtain. When times got bad, I told her, "I love you more than all the pebbles on the beach" - and I did.

68

My family was right. When I was feeling cranky and out of sorts, I tried to remember that it wasn't her fault that I had to climb eight flights of steps without any legs. I choked back my frustrations and decided I would just pull it together and be a better husband.

Everything was going well when something happened that would trouble me for many years. One evening I came in from work very tired.

After dinner, I showered and went to bed early. Connie stayed up to read for a while. Our apartment was about a mile from the Tulsa Fair grounds. When she was through reading, Connie turned off the light. As she was crawling across me to get to her side of the bed, someone set off fireworks at the fair grounds. Startled, I raised up out of a deep sleep ready to protect myself. My hand stopped about two inches from her face.

In today's Corps, they teach martial arts. In my day, we learned hand-to-hand combat. Hand-to-hand had only one purpose - to kill. In less than a heartbeat, I could have driven her nose bone through her brain.

I didn't tell her what really happened that night. She simply thought that I almost hit her. I let her think that. I didn't want her to be afraid of me. I loved her so much. It would be a very long time before I allowed myself to fall into a deep sleep. It had been a close call – too close. I could never let such a thing happen again. When she slept, I stayed awake most of the night determined to protect her, even from me.

By the end of the year, I began to have trouble with my prostheses. To get in the VA[41] system, I had to check

41 VA - Veterans Administration

into the hospital in Muskogee for three days. While I was there, the powers that be decided that I should go to college. After a battery of tests, they decided that I should pursue a teaching degree. We left Tulsa and moved to Edmond, Oklahoma, where I attended Central State College.[42]

I started school in January of 1967. At the end of the first semester, we took a trip to California to visit Connie's family. Her father had been transferred to San Pedro.

While in California, I told Connie I wanted to find Lieutenant Mitchell's widow Jan. After all my talks with the Lieutenant at Chu Lai, I felt like I knew her. I wanted to check on her and the baby. I owed it to the Lieutenant to make sure they were okay.

I knew where they lived. We stopped at a phone booth and looked for her name in the phone book. Sure enough, there it was. I stared at it for a long time, but I couldn't make the call. Connie offered to dial the number for me. I just couldn't do it. How could I explain to Jan why I let her husband die? I was the point man. It was my responsibility to protect the platoon. How could I explain to her why her baby girl would have to grow up never knowing her father?

_____

42 Central State College is now the University of Central Oklahoma

THE CALL OF THE WALL

Pain is weakness leaving the body.

The next morning, we return to find Brickie Bowman and my nephew, William Ronald Beasley[43], on the wall. I want to touch each of them - the boys I knew as a boy myself. They remind me of who I used to be - of who I was when I knew them.

Later, I sit near panel No. 2E, thinking back to that day in 1967 when I nearly called Jan Mitchell. I reflect on the flaw in my character that allowed that opportunity to slip through my fingers. I felt like I knew her. When little Erin was born, I shared in that with the Lieutenant. After his death a few weeks later, I should have taken care of his family but when it came right down to it - I couldn't face Jan. I couldn't deal with the fact that I let her husband get killed.

Thinking about Vietnam always sharpens the guilt that I have carried with me from the moment I regained consciousness in the Philippines. He trusted me with his life and I let him down. This failing influences the way I live and see the world. Lieutenant Mitchell was my brother. The honorable thing - the right thing would have been to make sure his family was okay.

"I'm sorry, Lieutenant," I say softly and look away.

---

43 The Army insisted on spelling William's fathers last name as Beasley so that when Fray was discharged he continued to use that spelling.

My eyes drift to the first panel to my left. I focus on a single name – a familiar one, though I'd not seen it in thirty years.

Charles Sides.

I am shocked!

It can't be. I search for a reprieve. Maybe it's a different Charles Sides - not the same one who went through training with me in San Diego - not the boy I last saw before I went to Hawaii to join 1/4.

Connie senses my distress. Together, we look up his name in the book to see where this person was from.

Oklahoma City.

I know it must be Charles!

He'd been alive for me all these years only to die the moment I saw his name on the Wall. My grief is intense.

His name is on the first panel.

He was dead before I ever set foot on the beach at Chu Lai.

72

Family

We returned to Oklahoma and I went back to school. One day I came home and found Connie crying.

"What's wrong," I asked her.

"I want a baby," she said.

My heart broke for her. We both wanted children and had been trying but so far, we hadn't been successful.

We decided to call the Baptist Boys Ranch to see if there was a child that we could get to know. They introduced us to two brothers. James was twelve and Jess was fourteen years old. We began visiting them on the weekends and kept them at our apartment for Thanksgiving, then Christmas and New Years.

When we finished building our house and moved in February of 1968, the boys came to live with us.

I spent a couple of years in college but I was restless and my heart was just not in it. I left school and went to work for Xerox.

We continued trying to have a baby but after several tests it was determined that we would never have children - another legacy of Vietnam. I was disappointed but Connie was devastated. It wasn't easy, but we absorbed the news and made our peace with it. Family isn't just about blood, we decided, so we found an adoption agency and filed to adopt a newborn.

Time passed and no baby.

I was no longer happy living a "photo copy" life at Xerox and I wanted a change. When our church asked us to pastor a church in Enid, Oklahoma, we agreed. On returning home in Edmond after the first service at our new church, we found a note on our door from Connie's mother. Actually, it was two notes – one in the garage and one on the door, so we would not miss them. The adoption agency had called and we had a baby girl - Teresa Kaye.

Soon after our daughter arrived, Jess joined the Navy and James went to live with his mother.

We pastored the church at Enid one year and then moved to Guthrie, Oklahoma. A year later, we received a second call from the adoption agency and we had a baby boy, Eddie Jr.

Our family was complete at last.

THE CALL OF THE WALL

For Those Who Fought For It, Freedom Has a Flavor the Protected Will Never Know

I vow that this trip to the Wall will not be my last. I will visit it every opportunity that I have. I'll visit the Traveling Wall too.

There are so many names and so many memories. There is no way I can digest it all at once.

There is no way I will ever forget those who bled and died for the country they loved or the families and friends who suffer their loss.

Student, Athlete, Businessman

At the end of two years at Guthrie, I took a job with the FAA[44]. When the children were old enough for day care, Connie decided to attend college. I thought it would be neat to take some classes with her so I left the FAA and went back to school. This time I got in the educational groove. Not only did I graduate, but went on to do some graduate work. I would be the only one of my family to graduate with a four year degree.

After college, I took a position at the VA hospital in Oklahoma City as a prosthetic clerk. In the early years, wearing my prostheses was a necessity. Nothing was accessible to a wheelchair. Until the Americans with Disabilities Act in 1990 forced businesses to make changes that would accommodate wheelchair use, even the university that I attended had no elevators and many of my classes were on the third and fourth floors.

Many people treated you differently when you used a wheelchair back then. When Connie and I went into a store, the clerk spoke to Connie and not me. When we went to a restaurant, the waiter asked Connie what I wanted. If by some chance they did converse with me, their speech was slow and very loud as though I were deaf.

At first, this made me angry and many times we left without receiving service. Over time, I came to understand that they were not trying to be rude. They didn't know how to deal with someone like me. Before

---

44 FAA – Federal Aviation Administration

this time, the public seldom saw people in wheelchairs without caregivers.

As I became more comfortable with myself and began to lose my macho attitude, I used the wheelchair more and learned to negotiate barriers that would stop most people. As this learning process continued, I discovered that with a little creative thinking I could do anything I wanted to do and much faster than with the prostheses. We have a saying in the Corps, "Semper gumby" - always flexible.

A group of us who were disabled joined some students at the University of Oklahoma to form a wheelchair basketball team. There were only three teams in Oklahoma so most weekends we traveled. Texas had four teams - Dallas, Houston, San Antonio and Corpus Christi. Kansas had three - Wichita, Topeka and Kansas City. I loved the competition - proving to myself and to others that athletics were not beyond my reach after all.

We lived for the weekends.

One of the University of Oklahoma women athletes broke her neck so we organized a fund raiser for her. We played wheelchair basketball against the National Champion OU football team and alumni. The OU team was comprised of all three of the Selman brothers, Joe Washington, Rod Shoate, Tinker Owens to name a few. The Sooners were no match for our team. We were the only team to beat them that year. This game was such a hit that it became an annual event.

Oklahoma had no track and field events so I traveled alone to Texas, Kansas, and Arkansas to participate. My first major competition was in Houston, Texas. I tied for first place in the pentathlon. A friend who took part in the meet went on to win second place in the wheelchair event at the Los Angeles Olympic games.

I also won the pentathlon competition at the Arkansas games and the famous Wichita River Run.

One weekend, the Tulsa team was visiting. I was late, and when I entered the field house, the game had already started. My friend, Gail Cox, had taken the floor in my place. The game had been going on two or three minutes, but when I entered Gail was lying on the floor. He had a heart attack. The ambulance rushed him to the hospital, but he never recovered. His family asked me to preside over the funeral service.

I continued playing the game for a few years, but it was different. I realized that life is more than sports.

I left the VA and worked for a couple of years for an acquaintance who was starting a business that was right up my alley. We provided driving and transportation equipment to handicapped people. Things went pretty well. He made the money - I did the work. Eventually, we had a difference in philosophy. The owner decided that he would cut essential services like installing hand controls and other items that consumed a lot of time and generated a small profit and concentrate on large ticket items. Since we were the only game in town, we could get away with it.

This caused a conflict between us. To him it was about the money. To me, it was about providing handicapped individuals with the opportunity to live independent and productive lives.

When I came home from Vietnam, there were so many physical barriers in public buildings that many handicapped people gave up and stayed at home, out of sight and out of the collective awareness of society. I wanted to rectify this.

This difference in approach caused me to leave and start my own company. Ironically, the competition forced my old partner to continue providing the very services he wanted to eliminate.

In the beginning, you could buy products but they came in a kit and you had to put them together. That's not always something a person with a physical disability can manage. That's what my business was - right at the beginning of getting people out into the world. I started in 1979, aiming to keep prices down and help folks as much as I could. Wheelchair lifts for vans were my main product. I'd buy the parts, put them together and install them.

At first, I took a small loan against my house to buy the necessary tools and basic inventory and I was in business. After a couple of years the business had grown to the point that I needed more space, more inventory, more help and even a second store in Tulsa. In order to do all this, I needed money.

I went to the SBA[45] and picked up a loan application, filled it out and sent it in.

It came back - they wanted more information.

I provided the information they asked for and sent it back.

---

45 SBA –- Small Business Administration

Guess what? It was rejected the second time.

They wanted more and different information. If they had simply rejected the loan I could have lived with that, but it felt like they were trying to make me look stupid for thinking that I deserved it.

The survival of my business did not depend on this loan but their attitude ticked me off. If I, an individual who lacked just a few hours having a masters degree and had two and a half years experience filling out government forms, could not fill out their documents in a satisfactory manner, who could?[46] I decided to make it my mission to get this loan. To be sure that every "i" was dotted and every "t" was crossed, I hired a CPA to help with the forms. This time I would not mail the application but hand-deliver it. I would make the trip in my wheelchair from my office in Edmond to the SBA office in Oklahoma City - a distance of about fifteen miles.

Connie called a friend who was a news anchorperson at one of the local TV stations and told her the plan and when it would take place. Linda in turn called several other news services. The AP and UPI picked up the event. The radio gave updates every fifteen to thirty minutes. In fact, a radio news person followed me the whole way.

We would later get newspaper articles from around the world. It made the front page in Dallas, Toledo, Oklahoma City and Ontario, Canada. We even received one article from Germany.

---

46 I was later told that they didn't think someone with my disability could operate a business.

When I arrived at the Murrah Building, the news media had already contacted the director of the SBA and he was expecting me. He instructed someone to meet me and bring me to his office. Connie and I visited with Mr. Robert Ball for about thirty minutes. He assured us that he would personally take care of our application.

Apparently, Bob Ball had been taking the heat from just about everyone. He told us that his father called him and asked, "You are going to give that veteran a loan, aren't you?"

Later, an Oklahoma Highway Patrol Officer who recognized his name stopped Bob and asked, "You ARE going to give that guy in a wheelchair a loan, aren't you?"

Endless radio and TV interviews, and invitations to appear on local TV talk shows followed my meeting with Bob Ball. I was asked to join the Governor's Committee on Handicap Concerns, to serve as a board member in organizations I had never heard of, and on and on. In just a few hours, I became a local celebrity. Everywhere I went people recognized me as the guy who went down the Broadway extension in a wheelchair. I began receiving phone calls and mail from across the country.

I soon learned that many of my fellow Vietnam Veterans shared my frustration with the SBA. At that time, the laws provided for business loans for Veterans of other wars but it did not include the Vietnam Veteran.

In the months to come, the Paralyzed Veterans of America presented my case before Congress. Congress eventually passed a law that provided business loans up to $100,000 to Vietnam Veterans. I never took advantage of this law, but if I helped even one Vietnam Veteran, it was worth the hassle.

About three weeks after my meeting with the SBA, the phone rang. The voice on the other end said, "Eddie, this is Senator David Boren in Washington. I am calling to let you know that your loan has been approved and you will get your money in a few days."

After that, I was invited to every political event in the area. People encouraged me to go into politics. The Mayor of Edmond heard a rumor that I would be running for his office. He called me to see if it was true. He said he planned to drop out of the race if I was going to run. I told him I thought he was doing a good job as mayor and I was not interested in being a politician.

It is good to know politicians but I would not want to be one.

I even played a bit part in a documentary film entitled "Breaking Through" about the difficulties of being handicapped. They had me riding up an escalator at the mall with my daughter, Teresa, in my lap. We did it over and over until mall security finally chased us out.

My business flourished. I worked hard to provide for those in need regardless of their financial situation.

One of the most gratifying jobs was for a young man by the name of Gilbert, a twenty-one-year old who dove into a pond and broke his neck. With his whole life ahead of him, his desire was to be able to live life without being dependent on others. Most of all he wanted to drive. He was told there was nothing that could be done for him. He only had the use of one arm.

I remembered figuring out how to drive while I was on leave from Oak Knoll for a funeral. When I came back to Oklahoma after leaving the Marines, the first thing I did was buy a car and customize it. I understood the young man's wish for mobility.

After meeting with Gilbert and assessing his ability and by using servo units and other custom-built equipment, we were able to build a van he could drive.

Another time, I created a tractor lift for a quadriplegic farmer. I never patented or marketed it because everyone has different abilities and disabilities. These are one-of-a-kind solutions. That's why I enjoyed doing them so much – each customer was a challenge.

By this time, our Oklahoma City store was doing great but our Tulsa store never got off the ground. I was unable to find a manager who shared my vision of keeping costs down so more people could afford the equipment. If they couldn't afford to buy it, we found a way to provide. It was not about the money. It was about helping a group of people to become independent and self-sufficient who, up until then, mostly stayed at home and depended on other people.

To that end, I packed up my family and moved to the Tulsa area. Since we were going to be there anyway, our church asked if we would pastor a small country church just south of Tulsa. We gladly accepted, as that was my mother's church.

Time went by and our children grew up, married and had families of their own. Teresa had four children - Dillon, Brittnee, Keith and Jace. Eddie had three - Tyler, Ariel and Kylee. Our foster son James had two - Stephanie and BJ.

As the Tulsa store began to grow, our customer base reached as far east as Little Rock, Arkansas, west into Arizona, north to Wichita, Kansas, and south to Wichita Falls, Texas.

Encouraged by my success, I began to envision stores in major cities in the surrounding states. I found a place in Little Rock and hung up my shingle. I was trying to save the handicapped world one job at a time. The business consumed me. I became a workaholic. I felt the weight of the handicap world was on my shoulders. People depended on me to the point of calling me on weekends, at night and holidays.

My health began to suffer. I saw my doctor. He began to run tests. For the next three years, he referred me to a specialist who ran every heart related test

84

available. They could never find anything wrong but eventually decided that my problem was work related.

The doctor ordered me to quit work or die. That wasn't something I wanted to hear. He told me if I did not quit work that I should not bother coming back to see him. I gave in.

Our managers ran the business until we found a buyer. We turned the business over to our kids and moved back to our home in Edmond.

The church Connie and I were attending in Edmond was having some problems. The pastor left abruptly to take another job running a homeless shelter. They hired another pastor who left after six months due to family problems. After some turmoil, the church asked Connie and me to help while they found a new pastor. We agreed.

THE CALL OF THE WALL

*Pain is temporary, bones heal, chicks dig scars and
glory is forever*

It's almost time to leave. I sit in my chair and stare
at the wall.

Death is capricious – so is life.

Brickie Bowman was having fun with a friend when
that tracer round found him. The other boys were on
their way to the showers when their grenades exploded.
Our company commander, Captain Sweeney, was
relieved of duty by Captain Dan McMahon as his time
in country was up. The night before he was to leave
Vietnam, Captain Sweeney fell off a cliff and died.

Lieutenant Mitchell and Corporal Duffy chose to
come through the bushes to the left and front of me.
That small decision cost them their lives. Sergeant Bolt
was safe at the rear of the line when I found that first
mine. Why did he come forward at just that moment?
Why didn't I see that second mine until it was too late?
Why were we sent out on patrol at all that day?

You can go crazy trying to figure out why.

Life can be confusing for the Vietnam Veteran.
First, there was the craziness that engulfed us while in
country. Then there was the awkward way we all
returned. At least I had some decompression time
because my wounds focused me on the immediate task
of staying alive.

I regained my awareness of external things while in California. I heard about people burning recruiter offices and protesters attacking wounded soldiers. Two of the guys from the amputee ward at Oak Knoll were beaten up in Oakland. For eight-and-a-half months, that was my reality. Like other men in similar circumstances, I was humiliated and frustrated. Then when we were home after the "conflict" was over, World War II and Korean War Veterans rejected us because we "lost" a war we weren't allowed to win. It's no wonder many Vietnam Veterans withdrew from anything and everything military, while others lived with anger and bitterness.

Connie is the center of my world and has been since 1965, when she walked into that hospital ward. So many guys in such bad shape overwhelmed her, but unlike others who chose to ignore us, she stayed - with them and with me. Her devotion and love has sustained me over the years. We choose happiness even when our world is complicated and difficult. Guilt, sorrow and loss are burdens I must bear, but after seeing death up close, I am grateful for the many joys and satisfactions in my life.

I see my own reflection in the black granite one more time before I start my long journey back home to Oklahoma with Connie and Dillon. After spending time at the Wall, I wonder about those boys who survived and are now middle-aged men like me. I wonder about Jan Mitchell and her daughter. Perhaps it's time to find them.

Reaching Out

Some things you choose, other things are chosen for you. One evening I received a call from Eddie G. He had read an article in his local paper about how our old friend, Norm Kegerreis, who lived in Pennsylvania was searching for Jan Mitchell. I encouraged him to contact the reporter who wrote the article.

I waited eagerly to hear that Eddie G had located Jan. I lay awake at night thinking about what I would say to her. I wanted to tell her that I had hoped and prepared for this moment, so I could tell her how sorry I was that I had not kept her husband and the others safe. I was point man. It was my responsibility. Most of all I wanted to apologize to her for not being there for her and the baby after her husband was killed. The nightmares and night sweats began to return. A life that I had tried so hard to put behind me began to invade my every thought.

The days turned into weeks and the weeks into months - still no word. As hopes of finding her began to fade, I busied myself working at the church and spending time with my grandchildren. As a grandparent, I have learned that grand children are God's reward for not killing your own kids.

Then on Veterans Day 1999, the call came. Connie answered the phone.

"Ed, it's Jan," she said.

As I came to the phone, I tried to remember some of those lines I had rehearsed, but my mind went blank. I couldn't remember any of them. I had no idea what to say to her. Fortunately, she lead the conversation and put me at ease. Before we hung up, Jan told me how to get in touch with her daughter, Erin.

I took a little time to gather my thoughts before I dialed Erin's number. I was apprehensive, to say the very least. Jan had told me that she had not talked with Erin much about her father and that she was in the process of writing a book so that Erin would know a little bit about James Mitchell.

Although I had known Erin all her life or at least known of her, she didn't have a clue who I was. I introduced myself and told her that I served with her father. I told her that the same land mine that took his life injured me too. Mostly we talked about her family.

After that, we chatted by phone from time to time but circumstances prevented me from going to meet either Jan or Erin.

Then, in October of the following year, Jan came to Oklahoma City. Norm drove in from Pennsylvania. He came in early so that he was with Connie and me when we picked Jan up at the airport. A reporter from one of the local TV stations was there to cover the reunion. We got rooms at a motel in Edmond and spent the next few days getting acquainted.

I was eager to spend time with Jan and find out how she'd lived through those first years after the Lieutenant died. I wanted to know about baby Erin who was an adult now with children of her own. I was eager to hear more about that book Jan was writing about Lieutenant Mitchell titled, "The Last Stamp: Remembering a Remarkable Young Man."

After that, I chatted with Erin a couple more times and set a date to meet her. I had hoped and prayed for this opportunity for thirty-five years.

As we got close to Durham, North Carolina, where Erin lived at the time, I tried to anticipate all the questions Erin might have about her father. I knew that Jan had questions. Others had tried to answer for her, but they were not there. They could only tell her what they had heard. Like Jan, Erin had a right to know the truth. I resolved to make my answers as honest and straightforward as I could. Anything she wanted to ask, no matter how painful, I would answer.

As the tension mounted, my phone rang. It was Erin: "Ed, where are you?"

"About twenty minutes away," I answered.

She had made reservations for us at a motel. She gave us directions. Her voice was pleasant and helped to lower the anxiety level. We checked into the motel and I called her.

It was late, but I asked if we could come over anyway. I had waited a long time to see her. To wait through another night would have been unbearable.

When we arrived, Erin and her husband, Scott, were waiting for us.

My mouth was dry. My hands were shaking. I thought to myself that I would rather be on patrol back in Vietnam than to do this.

I was nervous when I met Jan, but I was able to prepare myself for that meeting. Jan, Jim and I had all made our own decisions about becoming involved with the Marine Corps and those decisions brought us to where we are today.

This was different. This time I was meeting the innocent little "baby girl" who had no choice at all in the events that had taken her father from her before she would ever get a chance to see him. This meeting forced me to deal with all those things I had tried so hard to put out of my mind.

We spent a little time with Erin and Scott that evening, met their children and made plans to meet with Erin the following day. When we arrived the next day, Scott was at work and the boys were at school. Connie played with Ally to give Erin and me a chance to talk. I wanted to help her to know her father, the man who I knew and admired. It was hard to know if I was telling her all she wanted to know.

Later that afternoon when the boys got home from school, Erin let them go with us back to the motel so they could go swimming. What a great honor - that she would trust me with her children. Erin came to pick up the boys a little later. The following day Connie and I went to Camp Lejeune and bought them all some Marine Corps "stuff".

We watched the season finale of Survivor Outback with them - then it was good-bye.

On the trip back to Oklahoma, I tried to sort things out in my mind. For two days, I drove, hardly speaking a word. Connie spent her time reading a book. I had not been able to understand Erin. Had I helped or made things worse? She had spent most of her time making sure I was okay. (Just like her father). I had expected her to bombard me with questions. My niece, Gina, is the daughter of my brother, Gene, who died in a truck-train accident just a few months before I joined the Marines. Gina had not yet been born. She never knew her father. Every time I see her, she is full of questions. She wants to know every detail of everything I can remember about him. Erin, on the other hand, seemed to avoid asking a lot of questions or getting into any deep discussions.

On returning home, I was unable to get back in the groove of life. There were so many depending on me for so many things. Our church lost the pastor, so they asked me to fill in while they found a new one. The congregation had been hurt and needed a lot of care.

We lost our granddaughter and her mother in a terrible auto accident. Our daughter needed my attention.

Even so, thoughts of Vietnam consumed me once again - especially the day Lieutenant Mitchell and Corporal Duffy died. What could I have done differently? Did I make it clear enough that we were in a minefield? I had thought about this many times but now that I had met Erin and her family it haunted me even more.

Then, I was asked to be guest of honor at the Marine Corps Birthday Ball in Tulsa. I invited Scott, Erin and Jan. They were all able to make it. This was one of the greatest nights of my life. My fellow Marines honored me, but even better than that, I was able to introduce Jan and Erin to them and to see the tremendous honor and respect my Marines showed to the wife and daughter of a fallen brother.

Erin and Scott spent Thanksgiving 2002 with us. We had a big dinner with family and friends. Connie and I had conspired with Jan to surprise Erin. Jan flew in from Phoenix. After dinner, I made an excuse to leave and went to the airport to pick her up.

After more eating and visiting, Jan called Erin and me aside, away from the crowd. Jan gave Erin Jim's Purple Heart medal. WOW! What a moment.

If I would have written the script myself, I could never have penned this storybook ending - or should I say this storybook beginning. For thirty-five years, I regretted not calling Jan when I had the chance, now here she was in my home with Erin, Scott, Kye, Chase and Ally.

Lieutenant Mitchell, I failed you once but now that I have found Jan and Erin, I will be there for them and your beautiful grandchildren. Sir, I let you down once, but it won't happen again.

THE CALL OF THE WALL -- August, 2005

Semper Fidelis

In May 2005, Corporal Daniel Duffy's sister, Felicia, contacted the 1/4 Delta Company website. She left her e-mail address and phone number. David (Red Dog) Roberts contacted Jan. Jan called Felicia. Then she called me and gave me Felicia's number. I have been in contact with her by phone but have not yet been able to meet her. Soon my search that began with that first visit to the Wall will be complete.

As I write these words, I realize how blessed I have been.

I am not living the life I visualized when I joined the Marines. That seventeen-year-old boy is gone, but I'm happy with the man who took his place. Like anyone else, I have known great joy and great sadness. I've lived through pain and horror, regret and grief. I've worked hard, reached high and sometimes I achieved things I never thought possible. When success eluded me, I learned to stretch further.

It was terrible to lose my legs, but I do not define myself by my disability. When something like that happens, it amplifies your personality - it doesn't change it. There have been times when I've missed running. It bothers me that I can't race across the field with a kid on my shoulders, but I can't be angry. What happened, happened.

In fact, there's more upside than downside to my disability. Along the way, I've done things and met people who influenced my life profoundly. The Marines taught me to dig deep and find resources inside myself - things like pride, courage and strength. They didn't put those things inside me but helped me bring out what was already there. That skill still helps me. When things get tough, I "improvise and overcome" - a Marine expression that means "always have some control over who you are and what you are". When I was wounded, my first inclination was to panic. I recognized what was happening and realized I was going into shock. I could have let go, died right on the spot, but my Marine training took over. It saved my life.

The young corpsman, the doctor at Bmed and the chopper pilots also saved my life. I can't remember their names, but every day I treasure what they worked so hard to preserve.

There were others too. There was the young Lieutenant in Hawaii who gave me a chance to run and win. There was Charles Sides who taught me that working as a team and helping my comrades is more important than being first. Lieutenant Mitchell showed me that you don't have to be tall to be a big man.

Wheelchair athletics and the people I met through that venue allowed me to compete and win again. Pastoring gave me a chance to nurture a congregation. My business let me reach out and help folks with profound injuries, sharing with them things I learned. My doctor taught me to let go. Having a family, children and grandchildren completed the circle -and Connie - she gave me so much - love, compassion, loyalty - a life.

I thought I was ordinary, but thinking back, I'm amazed at the overall mosaic. I carried the flag when American and United Airline pilots came through Oklahoma City following the paths American Flight-11 and United Flight-175 would have taken from Boston to Los Angeles.[47] General Motors chose me to carry the Olympic Torch for the 2002 Salt Lake City Olympic Games. I've known governors and former governors. I've talked with United States Senators and Congressmen. I've met Presidential Candidates and a former Astronaut. There are VA laws with my name on them. Education laws were written because of me. To think that I was able to do all that is gratifying. I believe that most people have done more than they realize. We must believe that we are not invisible - we all have an impact on society.

My life has been one of extreme highs and lows and everything in between, but the bottom line is that I was lucky enough to be a Marine. When all is said and done, if you are lucky enough to be a United States Marine, you are *LUCKY ENOUGH!*

---

47 These were the planes that crashed into the World Trade Center on September 11, 2001.

The Vietnam War Memorial

The Wall, located in Washington D. C., is a powerful and awesome memorial to those who gave their lives in Vietnam. Two adjoining black granite walls, almost five hundred feet in length and over ten feet high in the middle, contain one hundred forty panels numbered from the east and from the west. On these walls are inscribed the names of the 58,249 people who gave their lives in the service of their country. The names are listed, without reference to rank, in the order the deaths were reported, the first in 1959 and the last in 1975. Since the building of the wall, new names have been added, dating back to 1956.

Jan Scruggs, who served as president of the Vietnam Veterans Memorial Fund and authored a book about the memorial, conceived the idea. The design architect, Maya Lin, wanted the Wall to tell the tragedy of the war. To show the Vietnam experience as a wound that is healing, she designed it as a closed circle. There are two arms, pointing toward other memorials in the National Mall (also home to the Washington Monument, Thomas Jefferson Memorial, Lincoln Memorial, Franklin D. Roosevelt Memorial and Korean War Memorial).

The Wall has indeed become a source of healing for veterans, family and friends of those who never came home, and a nation that was politically divided. Built under the leadership of the veterans themselves, it has become a source of pride for Americans. In its simplicity, it has the power to inspire those who visit. A tradition of leaving messages and mementos at the base of the wall has continued from its construction in 1982.

Although the war spanned nearly twenty years from the first to last deaths and it became a divisive political conundrum, the memorial is not political. It serves to heal wounds and educate those who visit.

For additional information, visit the web sites

www.virtualwall.org

www.nps.gov/vive/home.htm.

MISSION STATEMENT

Our goal is to offer hope and encouragement to injured American veterans and military personnel through personal visits and providing each wounded person a copy of **Lucky Enough**.

"*Lucky Enough* is a concise, personal description of the courage, initiative and mental stamina which enables an individual to overcome the most serious of adversities. *Lucky Enough* should be read by every American and become an important part of the mosaic which makes our country great." — Henry Bellmon, Former Governor and US Senator and World War II Marine

"Eddie Beesley not only puts you there, but makes you feel proud to be an American." — Tony Orlando, entertainer

Eddie Beesley has been spending time with wounded warriors returning from Iraq and Afghanistan around the country. He spends time with them delivering messages of hope and support. He gives them copies of *Lucky Enough* and shows them first hand that even with grievous injuries it is possible to have a full and happy life. He's able to do this through donations to Lucky Enough Inc., a nonprofit organization set up for this purpose. Our young people need our support as they return and make the transition back to civilian life.

Marines don't cry, but sometimes their eyes sweat.

To help Eddie in this work, send your tax-deductible contribution to Eddie Beesley, PO Box 605, Edmond, OK 73083-0605, contact Connie Beesley at ebeesley@sbcglobal.net for more information or go to www.LKYENUF.com

It's time to share YOUR story:

Your story is uniquely YOU! The journey you have traveled is a road map of dreams, challenges, joys and even a few disappointments. Your life has taken you over both the rough and the smooth roads, over mountains and valleys and you've even explored those off road experiences. In your travels you've seen the good, the bad, and from time to time you've had to face down the ugly. For those coming behind, you can help smooth their journey by pointing out the pot holes along the way. Good times, you've had them... Not so good times, there have even been some of them as well. But they didn't stop you. And in the end you came out stronger.

Now is the time to share YOUR story... When you're ready to put your memories, thoughts, and personal challenges on paper, we're ready to join your journey by helping you capture the details just the way you want them recorded for all who read your story.

We are *Camden House Books, LLC.* and we would be honored to help you share the legacy of your life-journey through the pages of a professionally written, edited, typeset and printed book. And if you feel your story is ready for the commercial marketplace, we can also help you with that portion of the journey.

Whether you have hand written notes or a typewritten manuscript, we will team up with you where you are and help you get to where you want to be with your story. When you're ready to tell your story, email me, **davehail@cox.net** and let's begin the rewarding journey of publishing your own book.

Camden House Books, LLC
Post Office Box 727 ★ Broken Arrow ★ OK 74013

 *My Wish Came True...*

On Veterans' Day, November 11, 2014, at the *Oak Ridge Theater* in Branson, Missouri, a long-time wish of mine became a reality. Behind the scenes, the Oak Ridge Boys, teamed up with one of my favorite charities, *Soldier's Wish*, to make this veteran's wish come true.

Soldier's Wish, a nationally known organization dedicated to making the wishes of our active duty, veterans and family members come true. Joining hands with the Oak Ridge Boys they invited me to the stage during their Branson concert. On stage, I learned I would be flown to Nashville where all the arrangements had been made for me to record a song with the Oak Ridge Boys that would help veterans in their time of healing.

Soldier's Wish made it happen. The experience was more than a wish coming true. It was an experience I will never forget. The trip to Nashville, the recording studio, the technical staff, and the Oak Ridge Boys and Soldier's Wish, all coming together to make this veteran's wish come true. And when the last note of the final session faded and the studio lights were turned off, I realized this was not the end. This was just the next step in my commitment to help our veterans in their time of healing.

Now you can help me make a wish come true for another veteran. Go to, **www.SoldiersWish.org** and read about how easy it is to help grant a wish through Soldier's Wish.

Use your smart phone and this QR Code to watch a video of the night the Oark Ridge Boys and Soldier's Wish teamed up to make this veteran's wish come true.